As you read this book,
May you experience the Peace of God!
— Phil 4:7

Victor Chukwu
08/19/2023

MAKING LIFE-CHANGING DECISIONS

VICTOR CHUKWU

WESTBOW
PRESS®
A DIVISION OF THOMAS NELSON
& ZONDERVAN

Copyright © 2023 Victor Chukwu.

All rights reserved. No part of this book may be used or reproduced by any means, graphic, electronic, or mechanical, including photocopying, recording, taping or by any information storage retrieval system without the written permission of the author except in the case of brief quotations embodied in critical articles and reviews.

This book is a work of non-fiction. Unless otherwise noted, the author and the publisher make no explicit guarantees as to the accuracy of the information contained in this book and in some cases, names of people and places have been altered to protect their privacy.

WestBow Press books may be ordered through booksellers or by contacting:

WestBow Press
A Division of Thomas Nelson & Zondervan
1663 Liberty Drive
Bloomington, IN 47403
www.westbowpress.com
844-714-3454

Because of the dynamic nature of the Internet, any web addresses or links contained in this book may have changed since publication and may no longer be valid. The views expressed in this work are solely those of the author and do not necessarily reflect the views of the publisher, and the publisher hereby disclaims any responsibility for them.

Any people depicted in stock imagery provided by Getty Images are models, and such images are being used for illustrative purposes only. Certain stock imagery © Getty Images.

ISBN: 978-1-6642-9491-2 (sc)
ISBN: 978-1-6642-9540-7 (hc)
ISBN: 978-1-6642-9492-9 (e)

Library of Congress Control Number: 2023904513

Print information available on the last page.

WestBow Press rev. date: 05/09/2023

Scripture taken from King James version of the Bible, public domain.

Scripture taken from the Amplified Bible (AMP), Copyright © 2015 by The Lockman Foundation, La Habra, CA 90631. All rights reserved

Scripture taken from the Common English Bible®, CEB® Copyright © 2010, 2011 by Common English Bible.™ Used by permission. All rights reserved worldwide. The "CEB" and "Common English Bible" trademarks are registered in the United States Patent and Trademark Office by Common English Bible. Use of either trademark requires the permission of Common English Bible.

Scripture taken from the Holy Bible, NEW INTERNATIONAL VERSION®, NIV® Copyright © 1973, 1978, 1984, 2011 by Biblica, Inc.® Used by permission. All rights reserved worldwide.

Scripture taken from The Message. Copyright © 1993, 1994, 1995, 1996, 2000, 2001, 2002. Used by permission of NavPress Publishing Group.

Scripture taken from the New King James Version®. Copyright © 1982 by Thomas Nelson. Used by permission. All rights reserved.

DEDICATION

To my wife, Esther who has been a great support and source of inspiration in this journey to purpose.

To my awesome kids – Shalom, Shiloh, and Salma, who remain a motivation for me to build generations for Christ.

EPIGRAPH

"The scariest place to be is where God is not, no matter how successful. The safest place to be is where God is, no matter how fearful."
—VICTOR CHUKWU

CONTENTS

Preface xiii

Introduction xv

Chapter 1 FIND GOD 1

Chapter 2 FISH BIG 17

Chapter 3 FLY WITH EXCELLENCE 36

Chapter 4 FOLLOW YOUR TIME ZONE 71

Chapter 5 FOCUS ON YOUR FOCUS 85

Chapter 6 FIRMLY MAKE DECISIONS 101

Chapter 7 FAITH IT 116

Discussion Questions 125

Notes 141

PREFACE

After many years of living, I've come to understand the value of making timely decisions and being accountable for the outcomes that follow. But let's face it, in a world filled with distractions, making the right choices is not always easy. That's why I wrote this book.

In these pages, I share my personal experiences and lessons learned about decision-making. From recognizing the importance of careful consideration to understanding the impact of our choices on our future, I offer practical advice on how to navigate life's challenges and make informed decisions that align with our goals and values.

I believe that this book will be beneficial not only to Christians seeking to deepen their faith, but also to anyone seeking guidance and inspiration in their life. Whether you're dealing with a tough situation or simply looking for ways to live a more fulfilling and meaningful life, I hope that the teachings in this book will resonate with you.

Whether you're struggling with a difficult decision or seeking guidance on how to make better choices, this book is for you. I hope that the insights and strategies shared within will inspire and empower you to take charge of your life and make decisions that lead to success and fulfillment.

I want to thank my family, friends, and mentors who supported me throughout this writing process. I also express my gratitude to God for providing me with the wisdom and inspiration to write this book.

May the words in these pages bring you closer to God and help you live a more joyful and purposeful life.

INTRODUCTION

"You were born like your parents, but you will die like your decision."
—ANONYMOUS

Life is indeed a series of decisions, and we are shaped by the decisions that we make, as well as the ones made on our behalf. One crucial aspect that we have no control over is the family we are born into, which is determined by factors beyond our control, such as genetics and circumstance. However, there are many other aspects of our birth that are the result of decisions made by others: where we were born, the hospital we were born in, and who delivered us. These decisions can have a significant impact on our early lives and shape our future. Ultimately, it is up to us to make the most of the circumstances we are given and to make decisions that will lead to a fulfilling life.

I remember the unique story around my birth. I am the seventh child out of nine children born to my mother. My younger sisters are twins. I was told the story of how the doctors advised my mother after she gave birth to my elder brother to stop having children. According to them, she had had enough, and they sternly discouraged having more children in the family. But apparently, my parents wanted more children, or perhaps I had to come into my family. So when Mom was pregnant with me, she would not go to the hospital because she was afraid of the doctors. She enrolled in the Faith Clinic, which was built and operated by the church my family attended at that time. The clinic was known for adhering to strong faith, instead of administering medical drugs during pregnancy and delivery. This was a very unique method. I was born in that clinic without complications. Glory be to God! However, after many years, the clinic was forced to close down due to complications that had become common among mothers. In short, I had no say in where I was born.

Life comes in phases. In the early phase, decisions are made for you. You are not a mistake. Your family is not a mistake. God decided that you will be born into that family for a purpose. Perhaps Moses wondered, understandably so, why he was born into a Hebrew family, yet, lived with the Egyptians. This was all orchestrated by God. Moses was born at a time when the king of Egypt decreed that all newborn males be killed. However, the godfearing midwives refused to kill the babies, so they were told to just throw them into the water. When Moses was born, his mother tried to hide him for three months, and when they couldn't hide him anymore, he was tossed into the water. It was not a mistake. Instead, it was a calculated move that was made to ensure the child's safety and ultimate destiny. From the natural perspective, he appeared to be tossed into the water of the Nile River, but in actuality, he was tossed into the king's family.

Moses was thrown into the river on the very day the princess was there. He was later adopted, not just into any Egyptian family, but into Pharoah's (the king's) family. Moses' adoption into this family was neither by happenstance nor mistake. It was divinely orchestrated. Moses needed access to Pharaoh's family because many years later, he would be sent there to deliver an important message to deliver God's people from slavery. He had to learn the Egyptian language to communicate that message to Pharaoh.

Despite the circumstances surrounding your birth or your present situation, like Moses, you are not a mistake. God planned your life, even before you could make decisions. Now, reaching God's designed destiny for you depends on the decisions you make when you are at the age to do so.

As you progress through life, the number of decisions you have to make tends to increase gradually. While it's often said that we can confidently make random decisions by the age of 25, it's important to note that the brain is continually developing and changing throughout our lifespan. As a result, there isn't a specific age at which the brain can be deemed fully mature. However, some areas of the brain reach maturity at different times during adolescence and early adulthood. For example, the prefrontal cortex, responsible for decision-making, impulse control, and emotional regulation, continues to develop until the mid-20s. But different individuals can have different rates of brain development and maturation. It is also important to note that many important decisions are made during early adolescence to the young adult age. During this period, you need to be very careful with your decision-making. These life-changing choices can have a significant impact on your future. Your future harvest depends on the seeds of decision you have sown.

Our God is unlimited and timeless. Yet, He gives every man the right to choose. In recent times, young people have argued why God gave us the right to choose when He knows the end from the beginning. This concept has been misunderstood by many who have taken to media platforms to ridicule God's plan for humanity. But the simplest way I explain this to young people is by likening the creation of God to the mastermind of an online video game. The one who made the game knows the end of every path. But the end depends on the player. If you play well, make the right decisions, and take the right path, you will have a good end, but if not, you will lose your life. Imagine the maker of the game standing next to you. Once you make a wrong decision and go on the wrong path, I'm sure he will warn you. Why? Because he knows your path will lead you to the wrong place.

God knows the end of every path you can take. But He leaves you to make the decision. If you listen to Him, He will guide you to the desired destination. If you refuse to listen, the outcome will be undesirable.

King Joash was allowed to decide his future when he went to meet Elisha on his deathbed. Elisha instructed him to open the window and shoot. Then, he told him to shoot the ground. However, the king only fired three times before stopping. Elisha was furious because the king did this. He had a blank check but did not use it to its fullest potential. This serves as a valuable lesson to us all about the importance of maximizing our chances and making the most of the resources we have been given.

Everyone will be given opportunities to make choices. What you do with those opportunities depends on you and the choices you make. The choices you make determine the path you take. The boy (popularly known as the Prodigal Son) decided to take his inheritance from his father and relocate to a strange land. His father respected his decision and gave him what he wanted. How do we know his decision wasn't the best? The outcome was bad. The Prodigal Son realized he had made the wrong decision when he saw the desolate condition of his life. Hence, he changed for the better.

> "The outcome of your life is a reflection of the balance between the good and bad choices you made."

The truth is we have all made wrong choices at one point in our lives. But we can learn from our mistakes and use them as steppingstones to success. The outcome of your life is a reflection of the balance between the good and bad choices you made. I can recall many regrettable choices I made, but I learned several lessons from my mistakes. They helped to shape my principles for future experiences. One of those days in high school, I decided not to go home directly after school finished. I had become a little more independent and I thought I could decide when I should get home after school. So, that day, I chose to follow my friends to play some soccer on a nearby field. I didn't realize that the environment was not safe. As we played, we were suddenly surrounded by hoodlums who hung around the field to drink and smoke. Before we could say much, we were stripped of valuable personal belongings. I knew I had made the wrong choice and never repeated it.

The point is that the decisions we make have a significant impact on the outcome of our destinies. Therefore, in the upcoming chapters, I will delve into each factor that can impact our ability to make sound decisions in critical moments. By exploring these factors in detail, we can equip ourselves to make wiser choices and fulfill our divine calling with confidence.

CHAPTER ONE
FIND GOD

"Our best chance of finding God is to look in the place where we left him."
—MEISTER ECKHART

The Oxford Dictionary defines purpose as "the reason for which something is done or created or for which something exists." We all have a purpose for which we were created and exist. And we have one common feature: the desire to fulfill our God-ordained purpose. God has a purpose for every man born on the earth. As He told Jeremiah, before we were born, He had a purpose and plan for us to achieve.

A man who cannot determine his purpose in life will pose for anything. Many have done this throughout history because they sought purpose in the wrong places. You cannot find purpose without finding God. Science can explain *how* you were

> "A man who cannot determine his purpose in life will pose for anything".

born, but only God can explain *why* you were born. So, if you want to find your purpose, find God. It is possible. The bible says, *"You will seek me and find me when you seek me with all your heart."* (Jeremiah 29:13 NIV). There is a common saying that explains the importance of God in our lives: The fish cannot survive outside of water for a long time because it was not made to. The tree cannot survive outside of soil because it was not made to. Similarly, man cannot survive outside of God; he was not made to. We are made in the image of God, and until we collide with Him and bow in surrender, we have not truly begun to live. God is the Author and Finisher of our purpose. Our lives start and end with God. You start, walk, and finish with God. It's beneficial to find a good church, mentor, school, or community to live in, but discovering God for yourself is even more crucial. This serves as the foundation for life and purpose.

FINDING GOD

At the very young age of seven, I was introduced to God. I was born into a very conservative church, popularly known for its strong stance on holiness and purity of heart. My mother was one of the top leaders in the church, while my dad served as one of the protocol officers. So, very early, I was introduced to the routine of Christianity, and I began to learn the rudiments of living a Christian life, though I had not found God. I was already in the choir and was learning the recorder, which is typically the first instrument you play to get acquainted with music and its vocabulary. I was somewhat like Samuel in the Bible, a young boy who served Eli, the old prophet, whose eyes were already dim, and his children were defiling the altar. One day, God called Samuel, and because Samuel had not found God for himself—he only served in the church—he ran to Eli when he heard a voice calling him. After Eli told him to go lie back in his position two consecutive times, the third time he became sensitive and directed Samuel on how to respond to the call of God. Thank God!

One day, the children's pastor called me after the service, and he explained to me why I needed to be "born-again." That is the process of accepting Christ as my personal Lord and Savior and confessing my sins with faith He will forgive and cleanse me from all sins (though they weren't that many at the time). I could only remember stealing my parents' coins and other people's belongings. But the day my mom found out; she disciplined me in a way I would never forget. So, I did not hesitate to respond to the call of God through my pastor at that time. He led me through the prayer of repentance and salvation. This is the first step in finding God. Yes, I was very young, and might not have fully understood the implication of the journey I started. But it was worth the start. It was the beginning of a lifelong relationship with God, despite many challenges on the road. Have you genuinely surrendered your life to Jesus? Many people are religious but are not regenerated. They go to church, get busy in the church, memorize the Scriptures, and conform to the traditions, but they have not been converted. Jesus said, unless a man is born again, He cannot experience the kingdom of God, which consists of His purpose and the possibilities.

SEEKING GOD

Being born-again is just the beginning of a relationship and a walk with God. Afterward, we must continually seek God to know His purpose for every phase of our lives. The ultimate purpose of our lives is to glorify God in every sphere He has placed us in. It is an accumulation of fulfilling our little purposes in different phases of our lives. Our walk on the earth is not without distraction, no wonder Jesus taught His disciples to seek *first* the kingdom of God and His righteousness. This act is highly intentional because surely, we will be tempted to seek many other things. We also tend to focus first on money, materialism, mansions, mighty positions, and pleasures. And once these things take away our focus, we lose track of our ultimate purpose on Earth.

> "The ultimate purpose of our lives is to glorify God in every sphere He has placed us in"

Growing up as a young boy, one thing I struggled with was my desire for pleasure. Like every other teenager, the hormones in my body were skyrocketing, even though I was dedicated to the church. But what helped me was my desire not to stop seeking God, even in my lowest state. David sang, "He lifted me out of the slimy pit, out of the mud and mire; he set my feet on a rock and gave me a firm place to stand. He put a new song in my mouth, a hymn of praise to our God. Many will see and fear the Lord and put their trust in him. Blessed is the one who trusts in the Lord, who does not look to the proud, to those who turn aside to false gods." (Psalm 40: 2 - 4 NIV) When I graduated from medical school, I pursued an internship job called horsemanship, compulsory one-year training required for all newly graduated doctors. The process was tedious, involving many applications to different accredited hospitals, getting letters of reference from multiple sources, traveling for exams and interviews, and praying for God's favor. On one such trip to a university outside my state of birth, I stayed with some medical students I was referred to for assistance. On one of those nights, a roommate announced he got a used phone from the market and expressed his shock at the videos he found on it. In our curiosity, we all crowded around him to watch the videos. Amazingly and unfortunately, there were a lot of porn videos. I was introduced to porn videos for the first time. I could not erase those images from my head. When I traveled back home, like a hapless fish on the hooked line, I was so spellbound I decided to look for more porn videos.

The Devil lied to me by encouraging me to watch more. He told me I was mature enough to see them because I was a medical doctor and had been exposed to many things. Well, at first, I believed the lie and engaged in dangerous pleasure by feeding my soul with filth. But on the other hand, I did not stop seeking God. I still had my morning devotions, attended services, and served in my capacity. One day, while listening to music (despite all that, I always listened to strictly gospel music), God caught me with the song "Awake My Soul" by Philip, Craig, and Dean. Read the lyrics of the song. I had heard this song many times, but this time, it sounded markedly different. I believe God wanted to start my cleansing that day, and yes, He did. Alone in my room, I cried and surrendered my heart to God for cleansing. He started to purge me of my uncleanness, and gradually removed my desire for porn. Later, I opened up about it to an accountability partner, which also helped me in the cleansing process.

AWAKE MY SOUL[1]

Awake my soul, prepare an entrance for Your glory
And let my heart become a throne for You to dwell

And when I need Your Holy Spirit more than life itself
Then Christ is formed in me

I told my story of transgression and deliverance because I know many young people, even adults, are struggling with one addiction or the other. The last time I did the research for a talk on pornography, I was shocked at the alarming statistics. I listed some of them below[2]:

- Over 40 million Americans are regular visitors to porn sites. The average visit lasts 6 minutes and 29 seconds.
- There are around 42 million porn websites, which totals around 370 million pages of porn.
- The average age that a child is first exposed to porn is 11 years old, and 94 percent of children will see porn by the age of 14.
- Fifty-six percent of American divorces involve one party having an "obsessive interest" in pornographic websites.
- Seventy percent of Christian youth pastors report that they have had at least one teen come to them for help in dealing with pornography in the past 12 months.
- Sixty-eight percent of church-going men and over 50 percent of pastors view porn regularly. Of young

Christian adults 18-24 years old, 76 percent actively search for porn.
- Thirty-three percent of women aged 25 and below search for porn at least once per month.
- Only 13 percent of self-identified Christian women say they never watch porn—87 percent of Christian women have watched porn.
- Fifty-five percent of married men and 25 percent of married women say they watch porn at least once a month.
- Fifty-seven percent of pastors say porn addiction is the most damaging issue in their congregation. Sixty-nine percent say porn has adversely impacted the church.

For many others, their all-consuming vice is an addiction to hard drugs, immoral sex, alcohol, and even video games. The Devil's tactic is to convince us with the lie that we are helpless. He says we cannot do anything about our human desires. And in believing this lie, some say, "I'm only human." As it happened to Peter, it happens to us. It only dawned on Peter that he was denying Jesus when he did it the third time. But thank God, earlier, Jesus had prayed for Peter. He told Peter, "Satan has asked to sift all of you as wheat. But I have prayed for you, Simon, that your faith may not fail. And when you have turned back, strengthen your brothers." (Luke 22:31-32 NIV). If you feel you are in a similar situation as Peter, remember that Jesus has prayed for you. Do not believe the Devil's lie that you cannot recover. Jesus expects you to get back up, and when you do so, you must encourage others as I am doing in this book. You can rise again.

Fervently seek God's face: "Seek and deeply long for the Lord and His strength [His power, His might]; Seek and deeply long for His face and His presence continually." (Psalm 105:3-5 AMP) No matter what happens to you, don't stop seeking God's face. Maintain a prayer and Bible-reading routine, even when you don't feel like it. Keep asking God for His strength, faith, and presence continually. God's strength lies in His presence.

LIVE SCENARIO

Mr. A (a young adult) reached out to me one fateful afternoon. He was so worried about his spiritual life. His desire for God had dwindled so much that he found it difficult to speak to God every day. He had developed a strong desire for immorality. His new environment was full of temptations, especially as an amateur teacher in a high school. He confessed to lusting after the girl students, who also dress seductively in the school. He was very far away from the closest church venue where he could worship with other believers. At this time, he had given up and was just ready to go all in with the Devil. But thank God for His mercy.

It is not my usual attitude to rush in with advice and counsel without asking the Holy Spirit to guide me. So, I prayerfully shared several things with him. I took him through the following:

Devotion: The Devil's tactic is to draw you away from the presence of God, out of the hedge He has built around you so he can strike you badly. My advice is to never stop seeking God, no matter how you feel. Maintain your quiet time, even when you do not feel like it. Keep praying to God, even in your mess. Don't stop asking for God's mercy. God is experienced in cleaning up messes. Don't stop reading the Bible. God will keep speaking until you hear. He loves you that much. Don't give up on your spiritual life.

Sermons and Talks: lust is a symptom and sign of a spiritual disease. Paul advised the Galatians to walk in the Spirit and they would not fulfill the lust of the flesh. When you starve the flesh, you strengthen the Spirit. And when you feed the flesh, it gets so big it chokes out the Spirit. Feed yourself with good messages and talks from reputable men of God. Let God direct you to the right people he can use to speak to you. Consistently surround yourself with these people weekly, and you will be surprised how God speaks. Once you open a permanent channel for God to speak to you, He will surely do so. The Word of God feeds the Spirit and cleanses and strengthens the soul. In Psalm 119:19, David asked, "How can a young person stay on the path of purity?" and he answered himself, "By living according to your word." The Word of God keeps you pure. Paul said in Romans 12:2: "But be transformed by the renewing of your mind." The Word of God is the tool used for the renewing of the mind. The more the mind is renewed, the more you are transformed into what God wants you to be.

Music: many young people risk the health of their spiritual lives for the pleasures of the flesh, and the outcome has never been pleasing. One tool the Devil uses to breed lust, sensuality, and seduction is music. It is not surprising that we have so many carnal and worldly songs with very nice rhythms, beats, rhymes, chords, and cultural streams but with demonic-inspired lyrics because the Devil himself was a musician in heaven. Every song creates an atmosphere—one reason why songs are sung in the church. Most songs invite the Spirit behind the inspiration. Be careful of the songs you listen to. Songs are channels through which spirits communicate with your spirit. Surround yourself with spiritual and heavenly songs; internalize the lyrics and let the Spirit flow through the songs into your spirit.

Remove triggers: one question I asked this young man was "What triggers you?" He confessed to always going through certain profiles on social media that he bookmarked and some other websites. He also confessed to being triggered by the ladies he was tutoring in the school where he teaches. The goal of this discussion was for him to identify these triggers and remove them. This is where discipline comes into play. It was difficult for him to delete his social media applications from his phone. But it is something he had to do if he wanted a change in his life. You cannot swim in the mud, and don't expect to be stained. Ask the pig! You must deliberately create an environment for purity, physically, digitally, emotionally, and in all ways. It takes discipline to ensure purity. There are many applications and types of software that have been invented by Christian bodies to block access to internet sources of temptations and lust.

Have an accountability partner: lastly, we discussed why he needed an accountability partner. He needed someone he could trust when he fell, not just to let the person know but also for prayers. Reaching out to the person anytime he fell eventually helped him to develop a stronger drive for purity, to avoid always reaching out to report. This can also be achieved by using software that notifies the accountability partner anytime the agreement is violated.

FULFILLING PURPOSE

In writing to Timothy, Paul said,

For He delivered us and saved us and called us with a holy calling [a calling that leads to a consecrated life—a life set apart—a life of purpose], not because of our works [or because of any personal merit—we could do nothing to earn this], but because of His purpose and grace [His amazing, undeserved favor] which was granted to us in Christ Jesus before the world began [eternal ages ago], but now [that extraordinary purpose and grace] has been fully disclosed and realized by us through the appearing of our Savior Christ Jesus who [through His incarnation and earthly ministry] abolished death [making it null and void] and brought life and immortality to light through the gospel. (2 Timothy 1:9 AMP)

Paul made it clear to Timothy that a life of purpose originates from the life of God. Even though the concept of purpose has become a very common subject today, it is important to know, as I said before, you cannot find purpose until you find God. Achievements in life can make you successful, but purpose makes you fulfilled. Not every successful person feels fulfilled. The worst thing that can happen to a man is having

"Achievements in life can make you successful, but purpose makes you fulfilled."

success without fulfillment. Purpose brings that satisfaction to life. Money without satisfaction can make a man miserable.

So, you might ask, what is purpose? In my definition, purpose is that thing God wants you to do at a particular point in time to bring glory to His name. The goal is to glorify God, but at each phase of your life, there will be a specific assignment that God wants you to do and finish. If you follow God's direction, you will notice a string of all those assignments. As you finish one assignment, you are linked to the next. They are all connected. A major part of your walk in life is discerning what assignment (purpose) God has for you at a particular time. Knowing this makes a difference in your life. When growing up, I knew some very intelligent classmates who helped others with their assignments. They were so busy with other people, they forgot they had their own work to do until a very late hour. So, they rushed their assignments and missed the details they would not have if they had made their work a priority. You must be careful in life not to be so busy doing other people's assignments that you forget what God wants you to do.

In my few years of life, I have had to move from one location to another, within the states and interstates, and across countries, progressing in life, and fulfilling my purpose. One thing I always want to find out anywhere I go to is what God wants me to do. Sometimes, it might not be what I want or what other people want for me, but it should always be God's will. I remember volunteering in my birth country to provide community services in a program every graduate must engage in as part of the process to prove he graduated from college. Another unique aspect of this program is you are randomly assigned to any state within the country to serve for one year. That year, I was sent to a very remote and rural area in the southern part of the country. I have never lived in a rural area in my life. The village I was sent to lies between several mountains and was known for hosting some Chimpanzees. I was really scared as I traveled there, especially as most of the journey could only be done by road. I had opportunities to relocate to a city or a town, but I didn't get the direction from God to do so. Instead, God kept giving me words of assurance of His presence in this unknown and very strange place. After one year, I was happy I had obeyed God. I ended up being part of a great family of God, featured in several concerts, became the acting pastor of the local church, had opportunities to impact and influence lives, and, as a medical doctor, applied my skills to save many lives. When I was leaving that village, I felt satisfied because I knew I had fulfilled my purpose. Yes, I might have gotten more money in the town or city but perhaps without fulfillment. <u>More success does not always equate to more fulfillment.</u>

Fulfilling your purpose requires following the plan God has for you. I used to say Jesus said "follow me" first before social media did. Nowadays, we follow people on Instagram, Facebook, TikTok, and other platforms. I am not sure how many followers Jesus would have had on social media if He were alive today. But when He called the disciples, He said "Follow me." You can tell that except for Judas, the disciples followed Jesus and despite the challenges, they fulfilled their purpose. Jesus kept to His word; He made them who they ought to have been.

We desire to follow God's Word, will, and way. His words are always true. His will controls the wheels of our lives. His ways are of peace to give us an expected end. As you follow God, He will make you. Your responsibility is to follow, while His responsibility is to make you. You don't have to worry about how He does it. God will mold you, activate the potential in you, keep you from the plans of the enemy, and elevate you to the position He has in mind for you.

> "As you follow God, He will make you. Your responsibility is to follow, while His responsibility is to make you."

CHAPTER TWO
FISH BIG

"Always dare to dream. For as long as there's a dream, there is hope, and as long as there is hope, there is joy in living."
—INVAJY

Dreams are glimpses of the future that God has purposed for you. Dreams, in this context, do not refer to the usual activities that go on in the brain while sleeping. Although dreams while sleeping could be a tool through which God can show you His plan and purpose for you in the future, in this context, it is not limited to our sleep. Dreams can come to you in various ways: instinct, impressions, insight, inspiration, illumination, illustrations through visions, or normal dreams. Dreams are pictures of future environments that do not correlate with your present environment.

Now that you understand the context of dreams, we can discuss this further. I believe good dreams are from God. God gave many people in the Bible glimpses of their future.

From a young age, Joseph had glimpses of the future. He did not have the details or the process map, but he knew people would bow to him later in life. David was abandoned to watch over the sheep, but he knew there was something different about him. He experienced God while alone in the bush with his stringed instrument. There, God revealed his future to him through inspiration. Moses was born in a strange time and was adopted by a strange family (strange to his roots). Despite being raised by a strange family, he knew he had an assignment and purpose in his future. He had an illumination for his assignment, but he didn't know how to proceed.

DESIRE YOUR DREAMS

One great step Joseph took after he dreamed about his future was that he desired it. It is one thing to have a dream, it is another thing to desire it. Many people have dreams that they do not want. To them, it is just a dream that may never come to pass. Joseph was the opposite; he wanted the dream to become a reality. The dream looked big and strange to him, but he believed it. In his innocence, he kept telling everyone about it. Yes, that got him into trouble, but his trouble paved the way to his destination.

Your desires are very important to achieving your dreams. They fuel them. Without desire, dreams cannot be actualized. When God shows you the picture; desire and frame it and put it in a place where you can see it all the time. God wanted Abraham to understand this process. He made Abraham visualize the dream. He asked him to look into the sky and count the uncountable stars, and He made the promise to him. God didn't reveal it to Abraham just once. He continued to show and repeat it until Abraham longed for it. That is exactly what God does. <u>He will keep showing you the dream until you want it because you must desire it to acquire it.</u> "Delight yourself in the Lord, And He will give you the desires and petitions of your heart." (Psalm 37:4 AMP).

As you take pleasure in the Lord's plan and purpose for your life, your heart is inclined toward it, and the desires for it begin to grow. Eventually, the Lord brings it to fruition. God is committed to doing what He has promised, and He has shown us. He is "able to [carry out His purpose and] do superabundantly more than all that we dare ask or think [infinitely beyond our greatest prayers, hopes, or dreams], according to His power that is at work within us, to Him be the glory in the church and in Christ Jesus throughout all generations forever and ever. Amen." (Ephesians 3:20 AMP)

FEED YOUR DREAMS

God gives us dreams in seed form. Before you plant the seed, you have a picture of what to expect when it is time to harvest the fruit. Most times, God shows us the final picture and plants the fertile seed in us. Your ability to turn your seed into a tree depends on what you do with that seed. Lately, gardening has become one of my hobbies. I have learned to plant young flowers and bare roots and learned how to tend them until they become full-blown plants. I must tell you that it is not very easy nurturing those flowers until they become what they ought to be. They need water, fertilizer, sunlight, and sometimes shade. All of these must be done at the right time and with the right amount of exposure. You must also study the weather, so the plants are kept alive through summer or winter. When God drops a dream seed, He expects you to tend it until it becomes a reality. Feed your dreams. God showed Joseph the bigger picture but dropped a seed in his heart. Joseph fanned that dream for many years until it became a reality.

> "When God drops a dream seed, He expects you to tend it until it becomes a reality. Feed your dreams."

Many years ago, while I was in high school, God dropped a seed in my heart. I was going to leave the shores of Nigeria to study and settle in America. I did not know how this would happen, or what path I would even take to make this a reality. I was only a young person preparing to take my exams to graduate from high school. One thing I remember doing was using my pocket money to buy time to browse the internet in cyber cafes (as it was called those days). At that time, Wi-Fi was very rare. Surfing the internet in the leisure of your home was something only the elite could afford to do. So, most of the populace would buy some time at a center and use one of the many computers available to browse the internet. Anytime I visited the cyber cafe, I met many young people who were using their time to watch pornography. It was very disgusting then but wasn't strange to many. It was kind of a normal thing. The internet was still evolving at that time, so it intrigued many that they could watch anything they wanted.

What was I doing with my time? I was searching for schools in the United States, reading about their requirements, and requesting school brochures. I had many school brochures in my home, to the amazement of my parents. I did not know how I would pay for the application fees, the fees for the entrance exams, or even the school fees. My parents could not afford that. It was also very strange to them. No one in my family (though I am the seventh out of nine), ever thought it was possible to leave your country to study in the United States. I remember when one of my brothers heard it, he thought I had lost my mind and maybe proud. He could not imagine how a small boy from a local town would make his way out of the country. Truthfully, everything seemed impossible. But I continued feeding my dreams. After a while, I expanded my sources of information to Canada. I started reaching out to schools there. I wrote to the admission officer at the University of Calgary, Alberta, asking for a waiver of the application fees. Surprisingly, she replied to me, but she asked me a very important question. She wanted to know how I would pay for my education for the four years if I could not afford the application fees. That was embarrassing, but I would not give up. I kept reading and seeing myself in one of the schools in America. One day, while I was reading the brochures of Yale University, I came across the symphony orchestra, and I envisioned myself sitting down with them, playing my violin. I just kept dreaming and keeping the dream.

Well, it will surprise you that I didn't get to leave Nigeria until about 11 years later. God always times the plan. It is for an appointed time. I understood later that I needed those years for more exposure and development of my skills before I could leave. While I kept the dream alive, I exposed myself to learning more skills to succeed in any environment. That's one of the ways to feed your dream. Open yourself to the necessary people and materials needed for you to succeed in the future. Don't stop developing your skills in any area. Be available to learn. God knows where He will be taking you and will open doors of opportunities for you to learn. Never despise those opportunities. In the Bible, before David got to the palace, he was learning and developing himself in the bush with the sheep. The bush was his rehearsal for the palace. I am sure he knew within himself that he was destined for greatness, but he had no details as to how that would play out.

David's proficiency in playing the stringed instrument proved to be valuable when he was called upon to send an evil spirit out of Saul and calm him. Similarly, his experience in defending his sheep and fighting against bears and lions proved to be beneficial when he faced the formidable foe, Goliath, on the battlefield. So do not despise your training ground.

By God's grace, I became a medical doctor and was able to sponsor myself to achieve this dream. Remember, your dream might be different from mine. It has nothing to do with changing locations. It might be starting a business or writing a book. Make sure you keep the dream alive through every season: winter, spring, summer, or fall until you see it bloom.

FISH BIG

I heard about a man who went fishing. Every time he caught a fish, he would measure it. If the fish was bigger than a certain size, he would throw it back into the river. Someone who saw him asked him why he did that. The man said that he only had a small frying pan at home. What do you think the man should have done?

Often, God presents us with great ideas and opportunities, but we may receive them without knowing how to act on them. In ignorance, we even reject or dismiss them as impossible. This happens because we refuse to acknowledge the person of God. "For as the heavens are higher than the earth, so are my ways higher than your ways, and my thoughts than your thoughts" (Isaiah 55:9 KJV). Anytime I read this verse, I relate it to the distance between the heavens and the earth. Just using the sun as an example, the distance between the sun and the earth at this present moment is 91.975 million miles. I know there are many other elements in the heavens, but can we use this to conclude that God's thoughts are about 91 million miles bigger than our thoughts? Do you see how our human thoughts are so infinitesimal to God's? God's thoughts toward us are so big. We cannot have a big God with small thoughts. I wonder what the brain cortex of God would have been like. So, when God drops an idea that looks too big for you to imagine, just remember who He is. He is God! He doesn't have to dream big; He is big. His thoughts are a reflection of who He is.

Another reason why many people ignore the big ideas and thoughts of God is that they fail to adapt to His plans. Again, what should the man who was fishing have done? Should he have gone home with the smaller fish? Should he have collected the big fish and cut it into pieces? Or should he have just bought a new frying pan? What if he did not have the money to buy a new one? Could he have exchanged the big fish for a bigger fry pan? Could he have started a fish business? (assuming it was legal to catch the fish and sell). So many adaptations might have been possible to accommodate the big fishes. When God drops a big idea in your mind, don't push it or just pray it away. You may have to adapt to your conditions to access the benefits that may accrue from that opportunity. Yes, adapting may not be very easy. It may require you to leave your comfort zone. It may force you to learn and do new things. It may cut off people you have been used to. Big dreams are very expensive. You will have to pay for them with some adaptations and discomfort. But one thing is sure: big dreams backed up by the big God always bring about big blessings. God said, "For I know the plans and thoughts that I have for you,' says the Lord, 'plans for peace and well-being and not for disaster, to give you a future and a hope" (Jeremiah 29:11 AMP).

FOLLOW GOD

Many times, those who receive dreams from God run with the dreams while leaving God behind. This is a very big mistake. God does not always give details, but He gives direction. It is not enough to have a vision or dream; you must also have

> "Many times, those who receive dreams from God run with the dreams while leaving God behind."

an implementation strategy to achieve the dream. Moses knew he was different, and he realized he was chosen to deliver the children of Israel from bondage and slavery. The only problem was he could not discern what he had to do to accomplish this. He made the error of going ahead of God in an attempt to execute the plan. So, when he saw an Egyptian beating up a Hebrew, Moses intervened and killed the Egyptian. This was the beginning of events that led to his exile from Egypt while trying to escape from the hands of Pharaoh who had issued his death warrant. Don't run before God or walk behind Him. Follow Him closely. Let Him guide you every day to your destination. There is a verse in an old hymn that I love so much. It says[1]:

> *Take time to be holy, let Him be thy Guide;*
> *And run not before Him, whatever betide.*
> *In joy or in sorrow, still follow the Lord,*
> *And, looking to Jesus, still trust in His Word.*

God loves His children so much that He would not leave us without direction. But many of us are so excited about the destination, we do not ask for directions. It is painful to have a destination without direction. Imagine how long it would take you to reach where you are going without a map or a GPS. A lot of time would be spent asking around and trying different routes with no hope of getting to the destination. God always directs while the Devil deceives. David highlighted this in Psalm 23:1, "The Lord is my shepherd; I shall not want. He makes me to lie down in green pastures; He leads me beside the still waters. He restores my soul; He leads me in the paths of righteousness. For His name's sake"

We also make the mistake of executing God's plan and visions for us with experiential knowledge. We assume the strategy, instead of asking for the strategy. Remember Jesus said you cannot put new wine in old bottles. I remember when I migrated to the United States as a student for my master's degree. One week into the semester, I got sad news from home that I would not get the promised financial support I expected to pay my school fees. I was very scared, anxious, frustrated, and clueless. I had no one in the United States, except for the pastor of my church whom I contacted on the internet. I was very sure God had made a way for me to come. I knew God sent me to that school and state for a purpose, but I didn't know what else to do. Honestly, I didn't pray to ask for directions, instead, I panicked. The only advice was to leave the school abruptly and go to another state to search for a new school. This was a very risky decision. I lost my student status in the United States and almost lost my legal right to remain. But thank God for His mercies. When I called on God, He re-ordered my steps, reinstated my student status, and reconnected me to my destination route. Don't assume you know the way to the destination God showed you. Listen for directions. In her encounter with the angel Gabriel, Mary asked, "How shall these things be?" She didn't assume she knew how a baby would be formed in the womb without intercourse with a man. She didn't just run to Joseph to give the information and start having babies. She asked the angel about the implementation strategy, and he answered her by saying, "The Holy Ghost shall overshadow you." That is the method. God has an implementation strategy to make your dreams and visions come alive. Download it from heaven.

FIGHT DREAM KILLERS

Earlier in this chapter, I stated that God gives us dreams in seed form. But as you know, they will not remain like that. Seeds don't remain seeds when planted in the soil of life. They grow and bring forth fruits, which is what God expects from us all. Jesus told His disciples, "You have not chosen Me, but I have chosen you and I have appointed and placed and purposefully planted you, so that you would go and bear fruit and keep on bearing, and that your fruit will remain and be lasting, so that whatever you ask of the Father in My name [as My representative] He may give to you." (John 15:16 AMP). Hallelujah! But you must remember that we have plant eaters that are eager to destroy your fruits (or the result of your dreams). The Devil also makes plans to ensure the dream God gave you does not come to fruition. But believe in God. "For whatsoever is born of God overcometh the world: and this is the victory that overcometh the world, even our faith" (1 John 5:4 KJV).

We can glean a lot from Joseph's life. His story was based on the dreams God gave him. The first people who attacked Joseph's dreams were his family members—his brothers. They were jealous, even though they did not understand what the dream was all about. It just seems strange that Joseph's dreams could come true, though an easy interpretation revealed they would be the ones bowing to him. Now, because of this, they wanted to kill him except for Reuben, who did not find it comfortable to murder his brother. The fact is that they wanted to exterminate the dream and to do that, they had to exterminate the dreamer. Sometimes, the attack on you is not because of who you are but because of what you carry and represent.

I experienced a similar situation. The first people who attacked the dreams God gave to me were those very close to me. The first time I mentioned the dream of relocating, some thought I was confused. No one in my family had ever taken that step, so why would I (the last boy of the family) ever think it was possible? My parents did not have tertiary education and were limited in the information needed to support or refute my decisions. But thank God, despite this, they kept asking to affirm and support my dreams and decisions. I remember telling my parents I wanted to do medicine and surgery in college. I wanted to be a medical doctor. Well, again, I was mocked and laughed at. I vividly recall when someone said, "People like you cannot do medicine." He argued that I did not have the education prowess to qualify as a candidate for this course. He advised me to focus on my church commitments and choose something that wouldn't require intense brain work. Again, the first dream killers are always very close to you, like family and friends, and you must watch them. It could be they love you so much they do not want you to make what they consider to be a wrong and strange decision, which is rarely always true though they might act like it.

As Joseph continued in his journey toward the realization of his dreams, he found himself in Potiphar's house where the presence of God made him prosper beyond his counterparts. He was then placed in charge of all the servants in the household. Now, this was not his final destination, it was just a bus stop. Many people would have thought this was the destination because at least some people were bowing to him. You can be your dream killer if you let your success hinder you from the best God has for you. Don't entertain imaginations that could limit your potential. "Casting down imaginations, and every high thing that exalteth itself against the knowledge of God and bringing into captivity every thought to the obedience of Christ" (Corinthians 10:5

KJV). What you think can either make or mar you. The Bible says as a man thinketh so is he. Paul also said that God can do exceedingly abundantly above all that you ask or think. Your thoughts are so important. They give your approval to the plan of God for you. God will not force you into your destiny. It is a collaborative journey. Another passage of the Bible says that God will grant you the desires of your heart. The good and godly desires are a reflection of the dream God placed in you. It is there encoded in your DNA in a seed form. As you interact with that dream, you develop desires, and the more you entertain and engage these desires, the more you bring them to God for him to actualize in His way. However, you should know that your desires can be corrupted if you don't bring them to God. The Devil can play on your imagination and contaminate them. Hence, you must cast them down immediately. Let me illustrate this quickly. As you might know, some people are in a vocation they didn't plan to get into but for some crucial reasons that might have great impact in their family or personal lives. For example, someone may have a sick mother who is dying of cancer. In the desperate desire to help, one may give in to the temptation to be involved in a vocation that is not biblically approved. The income from this act may help to provide good healthcare, but the source have been corrupted. This is the importance of taking your desires to God before it gets corrupted by the enemy.

A taste of success can make you relax, take down your guard, stop dreaming, and think you have arrived at your destination. But Joseph did not take down his guard. He knew God was taking him somewhere. The Devil knew, too, and used Potiphar's wife to tempt Joseph. If he was not sensitive to the plan and purpose of God concerning his life, he might have terminated his journey at this point. But he was sensitive, and he refused to sin against God. Sin is a dream killer. Why? Because causes you to deviate from the path of God. Sin blinds you to the path that leads you to your expected end. The Devil knows this, and he will create opportunities to make sure you sin against God, and also make you feel you cannot return to God.

> "A taste of success can make you relax, take down your guard, stop dreaming, and think you have arrived at your destination."

In my journey of life, at different phases, I was faced with a lot of temptations, especially towards sexual immorality. I was raised in a supposed Christian family; both of my parents were good Christians, but not all my siblings were born-again. So frequently, as a young and curious boy, I was exposed to immoral acts that were conducted in my environment. All these pictures followed me into my youth, and the Devil played around them for a long time. I must confess, there are times I thought I would just obey the flesh and do what I wanted, but God's mercy showed up. And the times I failed in my thoughts and deeds, God's mercy also prevailed. This is the confidence we have in Christ, that if we confess our sins, God is faithful and just to forgive and cleanse us from every sin. If you feel guilty and unclean and you think you have fallen from the grace of God, God's mercy and grace are abundant for you. Do not give up on yourself and your destiny. God knows how to reroute you to where He wants you to be.

Disappointments can also be dream killers. And Joseph had to confront and overcome this in the next phase of his journey. Your attitude during moments of disappointment plays a crucial role in realizing your dreams. Joseph was imprisoned for something he did not do. Be ready to face challenges as you journey into your destiny. God did not promise that the road would be smooth all the time; however, when you go through the bumpy roads, He will be with you. "When you pass through the waters, I will be with you; and when you pass through the rivers, they will not sweep over you. When you walk through the fire, you will not be burned; the flames will not set you ablaze" (Isaiah 43:2 NIV). While I was transitioning into a fearful phase of my life, launching into the unknown without a gaze of what my future would look like, God gave me a song by the Martins, "The Promise." That day, as I sat squeezed into a small car with more people than the car was designed to carry, I stumbled on the song and soaked in every word. See the part of the lyrics below:

THE PROMISE[2]

I never said that I would give you silver or gold
Or that you would never feel the fire or shiver in the cold
But I did say you'd never walk through this world alone
And I did say, don't make this world your home
I never said that fear wouldn't find you in the night
Or that loneliness was something you'd never have to fight
But I did say I'd be right there by your side
And I did say I'll always help you fight

Joseph's disappointment was not only about finding himself in the prison. God showed up for him there, but it was also compounded when the butler forgot him. Joseph met the butler and baker who had offended Pharoah and were put in prison. One day, they had a dream they couldn't interpret. But Joseph could. He interpreted their dreams. The news was not good for the baker, he was going to be hung on a tree. However, the butler had a good dream: he would be reinstated to his former position. Joseph asked the butler not to forget him, which, unfortunately, he did. Yes, some people you trust will disappoint you. As much as you have trusted people around you, it is important to know they can forget you. It is God who never changes. Immutability is an attribute of God, not man. So don't be surprised when men forget you, though it may hurt you. God said, "I will never leave you, nor forsake you" (Hebrews 13:5 KJV). The problem many believers have today is not with the promise. God made the promise. He never fails. It will surely come to pass. Even the Devil knows that. The problem is always the process. You must go through God's process to achieve the promise.

Be careful, the Devil also has his process; he may tempt you with the very thing you desire as a supposed reward. But in a real sense, it is a fake reward. It is not the real thing that God wants for you. The Devil will always show you a shorter route, like suggesting to Joseph that if he slept with Potiphar's wife, he would be promoted even higher. The truth is that it was a possibility; however, Joseph might have remained in Potiphar's house forever. He might not have reached the palace to take the position of prime minister. So, be patient, and follow God's process; it always ends with the fulfillment of God's promise.

CHAPTER THREE
FLY WITH EXCELLENCE

"Excellence is not a skill, it's an attitude."
—RALPH MARSTON

Excellence is the ability to do extremely well. It is the highest quality of success in any work. It is the end of the bar for good. The only challenge is that excellence does not have a definite point. Excellence does not have a constant measure. It is the pursuit of excellence that drives people to constantly improve and strive for the best in everything they do. The measure changes with time; however, it is recognizable and visible when it is featured. Rick Pitino explains it this way, "Excellence is the unlimited ability to improve the quality of what you have to offer." The mere fact that you exhibited excellence yesterday does not automatically mean you would exhibit excellence tomorrow. It requires a continuous effort to maintain excellence as you progress in life. Excellence can be achieved in a variety of areas such as academics, sports, art, and work. It often involves a combination of talent, skill, dedication, and hard work. It is not a skill that needs to be acquired but a habit that needs to be formed. When it is a habit, you seek excellence in everything you do. Excellence is often seen as a desirable quality, as it can lead to personal fulfillment and success in various endeavors. It is important to remember, however, that excellence is subjective, and different people may have different ideas about what it means to be excellent in a particular area.

THE SPIRIT OF EXCELLENCE

As a believer, it is important to also note that there is something called the spirit of excellence, which comes from God. As it is from God, the spirit should be operating in the lives of every believer. The ability to have the spirit of excellence in our lives is an advantage. However, only some believers give the Holy Spirit the free will to operate in His finest nature. Not everyone in the Bible exhibited the spirit of excellence despite having the Spirit of God. So there must be some other factors that play in the full expression of this spirit.

The book of Daniel illustrated the spirit of excellence. I encourage you to read this book repeatedly if you want to operate in that spirit. More than once, the Bible said Daniel had the spirit of excellence. Another version described the spirit as an extraordinary spirit. Excellence extraordinarily expresses ordinary things. If everyone in the Bible was not like Daniel, then there must be some other factors involved in expressing the excellent spirit. It does not come naturally; we must play a part in developing the habit of excellence.

DANIEL

Let's place a magnifying glass over the life of Daniel for a little while. The first chapter of the book of Daniel summarizes what we are looking for. Daniel and his friends were immigrants. They were taken from Jerusalem as slaves to Babylon by King Nebuchadnezzar. I would compare them to students who migrated from their home country to one of the top countries at that time. Now, they were among those given a full need-based scholarship to study in an Ivy League school. The first show of excellence was in the selection process. The criteria to be selected as one of those who would be eligible to train for the king's service were standard: "Young men without blemish and handsome in appearance, skillful in all wisdom, endowed with intelligence and discernment, and quick to understand, competent to stand [in the presence of the king] and able to serve in the king's palace. He also ordered Ashpenaz to teach them the literature and language of the Chaldeans". (Daniel 1:4 AMP)

Daniel passed this first assessment. The assessment required that his appearance, acumen, articulation, and ability were excellent. Despite his enrollment in this high-level training course, he did not forget his roots. He maintained spiritual excellence. He refused to take anything that would tamper his relationship with God. He was not distracted by others' decisions. He followed his purpose, and he was bold to do it God's way. He remained faithful to the word, work, way, and will of God. "But Daniel made up his mind that he would not defile (taint, dishonor) himself with the king's finest food or with the wine which the king drank; so he asked the commander of the officials that he might [be excused so that he would] not defile himself". (Daniel 1:8 AMP)

As a result of his spiritual excellence, Daniel had favor with God and man. Excellence opens the door to favor, which is an essential ingredient to succeed in life. Favor is when God changes the protocol for you. Favor is an unusual preference, unmerited promotion, undeserved grace, and unique attention. Daniel was favored in the selection, training, and end process. "Now God granted Daniel favor and compassion in the sight of the commander of the officials" (Daniel 1:9 AMP). It is also important to identify some factors that enhanced a life of excellence in Daniel. He had knowledge, skill, understanding, and wisdom. Knowledge refers to the information he acquired in all he had to do. You cannot excel in any area without first having the necessary information that is required to do what you have to do. You cannot build excellence on the foundation of ignorance. So, if you have the desire to be excellent in any area of your life: spiritual, financial, business, professional, or marital, the first step is seeking information in that desired area.

> "You cannot build excellence on the foundation of ignorance."

The next important ingredient of excellence is skill. Skill is a necessary tool to execute excellence. Skills attract opportunities. Unfortunately, they do not just come by; you have to learn and develop skills. When the Bible says God gave you the skills, it means He allowed you to develop what He had already deposited in you. We all have skills in seed form, undeveloped. You will be surprised when you take the time to develop your skills. Everyone in the Bible who demonstrated excellence had skills. The skills were the vehicles through which they executed excellence. I'll mention some of these characters later in this chapter. Certainly, Daniel developed his skills to execute his job excellently, and he rose so fast up the ladder that he became one of the three presidents in the land. He was also so skillful and valuable that he remained in the cabinet of a foreign government for a long time. He outlasted many kings. "As for these four young men, God gave them knowledge and skill in all literature and wisdom; and Daniel had understanding in all visions and dreams" (Daniel 1:17).

Daniel also had understanding, which is another ingredient for excellence. Information is not discriminatory. Everyone can and should have access to information. What differentiates an excellent person is the ability to understand, and not just to understand but also to have a deeper understanding like Daniel. He had an understanding ten times better than others. He also had a specialized understanding of dreams and visions. Understanding is beyond getting information; it is receiving inspiration about what you are doing. What produces exceptional results is understanding with inspiration. Many people have access to information. They receive hours of lectures, training, and tutoring, but those who have pioneered inventions and new strides are the ones with a deep understanding of the subjects. Daniel was such a person, and this distinguished him among the people who were given the same opportunities to learn like him.

The last ingredient Daniel manifested was wisdom. As the Bible says, wisdom is the principal thing. Wisdom is the application of understood knowledge. Daniel demonstrated wisdom in his relationships and reasoning, and it showed in his results. He related to his supervisor (Melzar) at that time with wisdom and intelligence. Melzar, who was scared Daniel and his friends would not meet the expectation to pass the test, had to rely on Daniel's explanation. We need the wisdom to pass across information and create and foster an environment that will enhance factors for our excellence. Daniel knew what he wanted. He knew the steps he would take to achieve excellent results. And with wisdom, he was able to push those factors in his favor. Daniel's ability to demonstrate wisdom did not stop at the first level; it continued in his life until he died. His results always spoke for him.

VALUE EXCELLENCE

In my few years of life, I have been privileged to work and meet different groups of people in various spheres. One thing I have observed is that the lifestyle of excellence cannot be exhibited by those who do not value it. Those who do not value excellence will always find a way to work against it. You cannot pursue what you do not value.

> "Those who do not value excellence will always find a way to work against it. You cannot pursue what you do not value."

When you do not value excellence, you will find it easy to debunk and destroy any structure that has been built to foster it. Yes, of course, there are many reasons why people do not value excellence. But many times, it is just for the sake of ignorance and the refusal to see any worth it brings.

I have had many privileges to direct and train various choir groups, in various church locations, under the leadership of various pastors. Many times, I have been challenged by the steps and structures I laid down to achieve excellence. Other times, I have had to forgo my plans because the leaders saw no need to carry them out. Unfortunately, even when you have built a system of excellence, those who do not value that system will work against it and bring it down.

So, it is important to appreciate excellence. Don't overlook it. Recognize; evaluate; identify and adopt any system of excellence around you. The more you value excellence, the more you are prone to render and attract excellent services.

THINK EXCELLENCE

Charles R. Swindoll said, "The secret of living a life of excellence is merely a matter of thinking thoughts of excellence. Really, it's a matter of programming our minds with the kind of information that will set us free."

I served as the president of a church group of young adults across various states in the United States for a couple of years. One thing I always emphasized while planning for conferences is that the planning committee thinks about the conference. I always tell them not to be afraid of thinking about the conference individually before coming to the planning meeting. I have noticed that if you think about the program, along with the Holy Spirit's guidance, you are surprised at the inspiration, innovations, and intuitions you have about that program. I always discouraged people from showing up at the conference planning meeting without having had some thoughts about the program. There should be individual insight and contribution to the planning of the conference. It is at this point of thinking that many inventions are born.

Excellence is not defined by your physical environment but by your mental environment. It doesn't matter where you are in the world, if you do not value excellence, you will not recognize it, and you will not think about it. Before I traveled to America, I valued the level of excellence I saw in everything projected about the country. I never once thought anyone living in America would not exhibit a life of excellence. But to my amazement, I realized that location is not the determinant of an excellent lifestyle. I came across some people who were very comfortable living below the life of mediocrity and had no desire or plans to elevate themselves.

> "Excellence is not defined by your physical environment but by your mental environment."

LEARN EXCELLENCE

As we have discussed, excellence is learned. You do not achieve excellence automatically. Some factors help you achieve excellence. We saw them in the life of Daniel, and in many others who demonstrated this quality. A life of excellence is anchored on four points: knowledge, skill, understanding, and wisdom.

Knowledge

Knowledge is a collection of information, facts, and skills that have been acquired through learning and experience. It can include both a practical and theoretical understanding of a subject, as well as the ability to apply that understanding in various contexts. There are many different types of knowledge, including declarative knowledge, which refers to factual information that can be stated or declared, such as the capital of a country. Procedural knowledge refers to knowledge of how to do something: how to perform a task or solve a problem. Conceptual knowledge refers to an understanding of abstract concepts or ideas: mathematical principles or scientific theories. Experiential knowledge refers to knowledge gained through personal experiences or observations. Gaining knowledge typically involves a combination of learning from others: through formal education or interactions with others and learning through personal experience and experimentation.

Your level of excellence cannot go beyond the level of your exposure and acquisition of knowledge. This is one reason why the level of excellence is graded differently by various people. Solomon built the first temple of the Jews, but it was destroyed 400 years later by the King of Babylon, Nebuchadnezzar. Then, the temple was rebuilt many years later. After the completion of the new temple's foundation, the younger ones who had not seen the first temple rejoiced and were very happy to see the progress. But the older priests, Levites, and other leaders wept aloud because they had seen the first temple's foundation. Though there is a mixed interpretation as to why the old people cried. Some say it was because they saw the first and thought the second was inferior. Others thought they might have been expressing their joy by crying that finally another temple was rebuilt. But if we go with the former interpretation, then it is because of two levels of exposure. The younger people who didn't have the opportunity to see the first temple were satisfied with the quality of what they saw, while the older people were not. So, your level of exposure determines your level of excellence.

There are many ways to expose yourself to knowledge. The most effective method often depends on the type of knowledge you are seeking and your learning style. Some common ways to gain knowledge include:

Formal education: this can include traditional schooling such as attending a university or college or taking online courses. Formal education can provide a structured and comprehensive approach to learning, as well as the opportunity to interact with teachers and other students. Daniel acquired knowledge through formal education at the University of Babylon. He was selected from many to train, learn, and acquire the information needed to succeed in the kingdom of Babylon.

Having a structured and organized curriculum helps you to follow up on your progress, test your level of knowledge, and improve your discipline. This is not always a requirement for excellence. I know people who are very educated but do not exhibit excellence. However, evidence shows that structure and an organized curriculum are big factors in displaying a level of excellence. A study conducted by the National Center for Education Statistics found that schools with structured curricula and high expectations for student achievement had higher average scores on standardized tests.[2] Also, a review of the research on effective teaching practices found that teachers who use an organized and well-structured curriculum are more effective in promoting student learning than those who use a less structured approach.[3] Sometimes, you may need to be exposed to that level of education to be equipped for the assignment God has for you. Moses was not born in Egypt by mistake. God knew he would be used to deliver the children of Israel in the future. So, he had to be taken through the system of Egypt, to learn the language and protocols needed for him after many years.

Self-study: this involves independently learning about a

subject on your own, using resources such as books, websites, and videos. Self-study can be a flexible and cost-effective way to learn, but it requires motivation and self-discipline. The Bible noted that Daniel also did a lot of self-studying. "In the first year of his reign I Daniel understood by books the number of the years, whereof the word of the Lord came to Jeremiah the prophet, that he would accomplish seventy years in the desolations of Jerusalem" (Daniel 9:2 KJV).

Daniel must have accrued many hours of self-study before he attained the level of knowledge, he needed to understand the times and plan God had for the children of Israel. One of the many things that have helped me in life is being exposed to material by people I look up to. I watch videos, listen to podcasts, and read books by renowned authors, especially those I have identified as great blessings to me. The internet has made self-study even easier today. You can identify and watch YouTube videos, take online courses, follow people you love on social media platforms, and learn from them. The world has become a global village. So, there are no more excuses for not being exposed to excellence.

There are also many examples of those who self-studied and excelled in life. Benjamin Franklin was a self-educated polymath who excelled in many fields, including science, writing, and politics. He is considered one of the Founding Fathers of the United States and is known for his contributions to the fields of electricity, mathematics, and science. Abraham

Lincoln is another example of someone who self-studied and achieved great success. Lincoln was a lawyer and statesman who served as the 16th President of the United States. He is known for his leadership during the American Civil War and his role in the abolition of slavery. Albert Einstein is perhaps the most well-known example of someone who self-studied and excelled. Einstein was a theoretical physicist known for his theory of relativity and his contributions to the development of the atomic bomb. Bill Gates is another well-known figure who self-studied and achieved great success. Gates is the co-founder of Microsoft, one of the world's largest and most successful technology companies. He is known for his work in computer programming and business. Mark Zuckerberg is the co-founder and CEO of Facebook, one of the world's largest social media platforms. He taught himself computer programming and used his skills to create Facebook, which has had a major impact on the way people communicate and connect. These are just a few examples of people who self-studied and excelled in their respective fields. You can achieve great success through self-study and determination, no matter what field you are interested in.

Experiential learning: this involves learning through hands-on experiences: internships, apprenticeships, or volunteering. Experiential learning can provide practical skills and knowledge that may not be possible to gain through traditional forms of education. This was so evident in my training as a medical student. I spent about ten years in medical school, which was unusually longer than normal due to many bouts of strikes by government workers. I should have spent just about seven years according to the curriculum. As I said previously, after medical school training, we are mandated to complete one year of internship, commonly called housemanship, where we acquire hands-on experience of all we have learned in medical school. This is where it became clear that learning theory is so different from practical. It was a new and extremely demanding experience. But after one year, I was more confident about being a medical doctor. It was not just textbook knowledge but also experiential knowledge.

Another way to be involved in experiential learning is to serve others. Service does not require expertise but commitment. In service, we acquire experience, get exposed to multiple scenarios, increase knowledge, and improve the skills needed to be excellent. The only issue with the millennial and the Z generation is that commitment and loyalty are not their key attributes. Without a commitment to what we do, it is difficult to attain what is necessary to achieve excellence.

> "Without a commitment to what we do, it is difficult to attain what is necessary to achieve excellence."

Social learning: this involves learning from others, such as through discussions with friends, colleagues, or mentors. Social learning can be a valuable source of knowledge and perspective, as well as an opportunity to collaborate and problem-solve with others. I learned violin at the age of nine through my church choir. I was in the first youth symphony orchestra that was formed in the church. Before then, we only had an orchestra made up of recorder players. So, I grew up playing the violin, until by God's grace, I became one of the top players in the orchestra (well, so I thought). After many years, my elder brother and I (who was also the best on the flute in our orchestra) decided to visit the Music School of Nigeria (MUSON) in a bid to join their symphony orchestra. Well, in the first rehearsal, I watched how the music sheets were shared with everyone, and in about ten minutes, the director summoned everyone, counted the entry beats, and they all started playing. I was taken by surprise. I had never been to a place where people could sight-play a new song in a few minutes. So, even though I was one of the best in my church then, I was put in the lowest grade in this new orchestra. The same thing happened to my brother. In fact, in some of the performances, we had to play percussion, an instrument so far from our initial plan. But this was a turning point in my violin playing. Because I was exposed to this new environment, a new standard of excellence was set for me to attain. I had a new challenge that inspired me to practice more to become better.

There are also many examples of those who have excelled through social learning. One example is Albert Einstein, who is widely recognized as one of the most brilliant and influential scientists in history. Einstein was a strong believer in the power of social learning, and he credited much of his success to the conversations and debates he had with his colleagues and mentors. Einstein was known for his ability to engage in deep and meaningful discussions with others, which allowed him to learn from their perspectives and experiences and to develop and refine his ideas.

Another example is Steve Jobs, co-founder of Apple and one of the most successful and innovative business leaders of all time. Jobs was known for his ability to surround himself with talented and dedicated people, and he was a master at encouraging collaboration and fostering a culture of continuous learning and innovation within his company. He believed that social learning was essential for success, and he encouraged his team members to share their ideas and insights, which helped to create a dynamic and forward-thinking environment. There are countless other examples of individuals who have excelled through social learning, including leaders in fields such as education, politics, and the arts. The key to success through social learning is to be open to learning from others, to actively seek new experiences and perspectives, and to be willing to engage in meaningful dialogue and collaboration with others.

The Bible also records a number of those who excelled through social learning. One example is Solomon who was known for his wisdom and ability to make fair decisions.

Solomon was known for seeking the counsel of others and asking for their advice and guidance. He often gathered together a group of wise men to help him make important decisions. Solomon's willingness to learn from others and seek their wisdom played a key role in his success as a leader.

Esther, a Jewish queen in ancient Persia is another example. She used her influence and her relationships with others to save her people from being killed by the king's evil advisor. Esther learned from her uncle Mordecai and others, and she used her social connections, wisdom, and courage to plead with the king and save her people.

There are many other examples of social learning in the Bible, including Joseph, Daniel, and Paul, who all learned from others and used their relationships and connections to achieve great things. The Bible teaches that seeking wisdom and guidance from others is an important part of personal and spiritual growth. It encourages us to be open to learning from others and seek the counsel and guidance of those who are wiser and more experienced.

Understanding

Understanding is the ability to comprehend and make sense of something, typically by interpreting and connecting pieces of information and ideas. It involves more than just knowing or memorizing facts. It is having a deeper level of comprehension and insight into a subject. Understanding often involves the ability to relate new information to what you already know and to apply that knowledge in meaningful ways. It is also being able to explain and communicate your understanding of a subject to others. For example, understanding a math concept is not only being able to solve problems using that concept but also explaining how and why the concept works and how it relates to other math concepts. Understanding a historical event is not only knowing the facts of what happened but also placing it in context and understanding its broader implications and significance.

You can understand a subject in several ways:

- Engage with the material: actively read, listen, or participate in discussions about the subject. By actively engaging with the material, you can better grasp the key concepts and ideas and start to build your understanding.
- Practice applying what you have learned: by applying what you have learned to new situations, you can deepen your understanding of the subject and better retain the information. This can involve solving problems, completing exercises, or working on projects related to the subject.
- Seek clarification and ask questions: if you are unsure about something or don't fully understand, ask for

clarification, or seek additional information. This can involve asking a teacher, mentor, or colleague, or doing further research on your own.
- Reflect on what you have learned: taking time to reflect on what you have learned can help you consolidate your understanding and better retain the information. You might do this by writing about what you have learned, discussing it with others, or simply thinking about it on your own.

Ultimately, gaining understanding involves actively engaging with the material, practicing what you have learned, seeking clarification, and asking questions when needed. It also requires persistence and a willingness to continue learning and growing in knowledge over time.

There are many examples of individuals who have excelled due to their ability to understand and learn new concepts and ideas. Daniel was known for his ability to interpret dreams and understand the meaning of visions. Daniel's understanding of spiritual matters played a key role in his success as a leader and a prophet. Paul, a missionary, and apostle in the New Testament, had a deep understanding of the teachings of Jesus and the principles of the Christian faith. Paul used his understanding to spread the message of Jesus and to establish churches throughout the Roman Empire. Joseph was known for his ability to interpret dreams and understand the will of God. Joseph's understanding played a key role in his success as a leader and a provider for his family. Moses was chosen by God to lead the Israelites out of slavery in Egypt. Moses had a deep understanding of the will and the laws of God, which he used to guide and lead His people. Nehemiah rebuilt the walls of Jerusalem and restored the city to its former glory. Nehemiah had a strong understanding of the plans and purposes of God, which he used to guide and lead the rebuilding effort. Esther was chosen by God to be the queen of Persia and save her people from being killed by the king's evil advisor. Esther had a deep understanding of the will of God and the role she was called to play, which she used to achieve great things. David was known for his understanding of the will of God and his faith in Him. David's understanding played a key role in his success as a leader and a warrior, and it helped him to overcome many challenges and obstacles.

In terms of contemporary examples, Marie Curie, a pioneering scientist who made major discoveries in the fields of physics and chemistry, was known for her deep understanding of scientific concepts and her ability to apply her knowledge to make important discoveries. Isaac Newton was a famous mathematician and scientist who is known for his work on calculus and the laws of motion. Newton had a strong understanding of mathematical and scientific concepts, which allowed him to make important contributions to the fields of mathematics and physics. Mahatma Gandhi was a leader in India's independence movement and a champion of civil rights and nonviolence. Gandhi had a deep understanding of social and political issues, which he used to inspire and lead others toward positive change.

These are just a few examples of individuals who excelled due to their good understanding of various concepts and ideas. In general, having a strong understanding of a subject or field can be a key factor in achieving success and making meaningful contributions.

The Bible also highlighted the benefits of having a good understanding. Having a good understanding helps you to know what to do at a particular time. "Of the tribe of Issachar, men who understood the times, with knowledge of what Israel should do, two hundred chiefs; and all their relatives were at their command" (1 Chronicles 12:32 AMP). Having a good understanding also brings and attracts favor. "Good understanding wins favor [from others], But the way of the unfaithful is hard [like barren, dry soil]" (Proverbs 13:15 AMP).

Skill

A skill is a learned ability to perform a task or activity. Skills can be physical: the ability to play a musical instrument or throw a ball or they can be cognitive such as the ability to solve problems or communicate effectively. Skills can be acquired through practice, training, or education, and they can vary in complexity and difficulty.

Some examples of skills include:

- Technical skills: the ability to use a specific software program or operate a piece of machinery
- Interpersonal skills: the ability to communicate effectively with others or work as part of a team.
- Leadership skills: the ability to motivate and guide others
- Problem-solving skills: the ability to analyze a situation and come up with a solution.

Developing new skills is an ongoing process that often requires a combination of practice and learning from others. Some people are naturally skilled in certain areas, while others may need to work harder to develop a particular skill.

David prevailed over the Philistine with God and his stone. His ability to skillfully "choose five smooth stones out of the brook" played a big role in the victory over the enemy. The Bible recorded that David "shepherded them with integrity of heart; with skillful hands he led them" (Psalm 78:72 NIV). God expects His children to cultivate their skills and stir up the gifts He has deposited in them. As Paul admonished Timothy, "Wherefore I put thee in remembrance that thou stir up the gift of God, which is in thee by the putting on of my hands" (2 Timothy 1:6 KJV). George Herbert said, "Skill and confidence (in God) are an unconquered army."

How do you develop yourself and your skills professionally? I will share a few lessons.

Self-appraise

Know exactly where you are and compare yourself to where you should be. Be sincere with yourself. As Paul said, "For by the grace given me I say to every one of you: Do not think of yourself more highly than you ought, but rather think of yourself with sober judgment, in accordance with the faith God has distributed to each of you" (Romans 12:3 NIV).

Search for a Mentor in Your Field of Interest

A mentor is a seasoned professional who informally helps guide a lesser experienced person in a professional endeavor. Mentorship is a mutually beneficial professional relationship in which an experienced individual imparts knowledge, expertise, and wisdom to a less experienced person. Having a mentor helps you to know where you need to be.

You can also learn new skills by observing and learning from others who are skilled in that area. This can involve taking a class or workshop, seeking guidance from a mentor or coach, or simply watching someone else demonstrate the skill.

Set SMART (Specific, Measurable, Achievable, Relevant, Timebound) Goals

Study your environment. Understand your professional ecosystem. Observe the culture, expectations, demands, and language of your environment. One of the key reasons Daniel excelled was that he learned how to speak the language of the Chaldeans.

Seek Resources to Achieve Your Goals

Subscribe to knowledge sources that can help you develop professionally. There are many resources available to help you learn new skills: books, online courses, and tutorials. Taking advantage of these resources can be a convenient and effective way to acquire new skills.

Repetitive practice is often key to developing a new skill. By consistently working on a skill, you can improve your ability to perform it. Going back to my surprise at the Musical School of Nigeria (MUSON), after I finished that day with the orchestra, I scheduled a time of consistent practice to attain the new standard I had to achieve. Practicing with the right materials while watching others demonstrate them improved various aspects of my playing. Sometimes, we practice but do so with the wrong materials. So, it is not enough to practice, we must also acquire the right materials to do so. Also, if you do not compare what you are doing to a standard, you end up creating your standard, which might be far less than what is expected of excellence.

Seek out New Challenges

Taking on new challenges can help you develop new skills. This might involve trying something new or stepping outside of your comfort zone. I realized I was not as good as I thought when I stepped out of my comfort zone. I know a lot of people who have lost their jobs because they were too comfortable with their level. They were not wise enough to step up their work. It is not enough to be faithful; be wise. "Who then is a faithful and wise servant, whom his master made ruler over his household, to give them food in due season?" (Matthew 24:45 NKJV).

The faithful servant knows how to give the food. The faithful and wise servant knows how and when to give the food—in due season.

Be Persistent

Developing new skills often requires persistence and a willingness to keep trying even if you face setbacks or challenges. By staying committed to learning and improving, you can develop new skills over time. The reason why many people do not succeed in their endeavors is that they do not stay consistent. Walt Disney's success in the entertainment industry is largely attributed to his persistence and consistency in creating quality content. Despite facing numerous setbacks and failures, he continued to pursue his dreams and eventually founded the Walt Disney Company. J. K. Rowling's Harry Potter series is a testament to her consistency and persistence. She wrote the first book in the series while struggling with poverty and single motherhood, and it took her several years to get it published. However, she persevered and eventually became one of the most successful and well-known writers of all time. You must have heard about Thomas Edison, who is known for his persistence and determination in inventing the light bulb. He is famously quoted as saying, "I have not failed. I've just found 10,000 ways that won't work."

Schedule Evaluation Time Points

It is always important to evaluate your growth with reputable indices. At regular time points, compare yourself to your initial goals, and adjust as appropriate. Also, open up to feedback from other people, and make up your mind to implement important feedback that will help you to be better. Many people want feedback but cannot tolerate it. Feedback is not always palatable, even if it is constructive. I once was close to a leader who loved feedback but indirectly attacked the feedback giver. This made many people stop giving him feedback, though he kept asking for it. It is not enough to ask for feedback; you must be willing to accept it and apply it to your life or whatever program you are working on at that time.

One of the secrets to the success of my leadership when I was the young adult president of a church organization, was my ability to listen to and apply important feedback, especially after a conference. The truth is that people were not always nice. Sometimes, I felt those giving feedback were insensitive to the amount of work that was done before and during the conference. But they may not have been; they were just trying to give sincere feedback. To assist and bias our judgment, we always made the feedback platforms anonymous. There are top people in life who became successful because they had a system and structure of a good feedback mechanism. Jeff Bezos, the founder and CEO of Amazon, practices soliciting candid feedback from his employees and using it to continuously improve the company. This has been a key factor in Amazon's tremendous success. Sheryl Sandberg, the COO of Facebook, credits much of her success to seeking and listening to feedback. She has said that she actively seeks feedback from her colleagues and uses it to learn and grow.

Wisdom

Wisdom is the ability to use knowledge, experience, and understanding practically and effectively, especially in complex or difficult situations. It is often characterized by good judgment, common sense, and an ability to see the big picture. Wisdom is often thought of as a quality that is developed over time as a person gains knowledge and experiences different situations in life. It is not just about knowing a lot of facts or information, but rather, about being able to use that knowledge to make good decisions and solve problems thoughtfully and effectively. Wisdom is often seen as a valuable trait because it can help us navigate life's challenges and make the most of the opportunities that come our way. It can also involve being able to recognize and learn from our mistakes and have a balanced perspective on life's ups and downs.

Apostle James knew the importance of wisdom and recognized that God is the ultimate source of true wisdom. So he said, "If any of you lacks wisdom, let him ask of God, who gives to all liberally and without reproach, and it will be given to him" (James 1:5 NKJV). Importantly, James also noted there is wisdom that is not from God. Yes, it might achieve some results based on the assessment of men but not approved by God. "Who is wise and understanding among you? Let him show by good conduct that his works are done in the meekness of wisdom. But if you have bitter envy and [h]self-seeking in your hearts, do not boast and lie against the truth. This wisdom does not descend from above, but is earthly, sensual, demonic. For where envy and self-seeking exist, confusion and every evil thing are there. But the wisdom that is from above is first pure, then peaceable, gentle, willing to yield, full of mercy and good fruits, without partiality and without hypocrisy". (James 3:13-17 NKJV)

Bezalel, Hiram, and Solomon were some people God filled with wisdom to fulfill a particular purpose. God filled Bezalel with wisdom to help build the tabernacle. Bezalel was good with cutting stones, carving timber, and in all sorts of workmanship. Solomon sent for Hiram because he also had the skill and wisdom to work like Bezalel. Hiram was an expert in anything that had to do with brass. Solomon showed us that it is possible to ask for wisdom from God and receive it. But he also let us know that you can get wisdom from God and misuse it. This was what James talked about. Solomon allowed his wisdom to be corrupted by the Devil, which harmed his life.

There are several ways you can develop wisdom:

- Wisdom often comes from experience as you learn from the successes and failures that you encounter in life.

- You can also gain wisdom by learning from the experiences and insights of others, whether through books, conversations, or other forms of communication. This can include learning from people who have more experience or who have faced similar challenges.
- Expanding your knowledge and understanding by seeking out new perspectives and experiences can help you develop wisdom. This might involve trying new things, traveling to different places, or interacting with people who have different backgrounds and viewpoints.
- Taking time to reflect on your values and goals can help you develop wisdom by giving you a sense of purpose and direction. This can involve considering what is most important to you and how you want to live your life.

Ultimately, acquiring wisdom includes asking from God, and a combination of learning from your own experiences and the experiences of others, seeking out new perspectives, and reflecting on your values and goals. It is often a lifelong process, as you continue to learn and grow throughout your life.

DO EXCELLENCE

Now, it is one thing to know everything we have just discussed about excellence, but it is another thing to commit to doing it. I have interacted with so many people who can preach about excellence but have not taken any steps to put it into practice. We must go beyond just talking about excellence to doing it.

Start by setting high standards and goals for yourself. This can help you stay motivated and focused on achieving excellence. It is important to be realistic and to set goals that are challenging but attainable.

Seek Opportunities to Learn and Improve

To excel in a particular area, you may need to seek out opportunities to learn and improve your skills. This can involve taking classes or workshops, seeking guidance from a mentor or coach, or simply practicing regularly.

Practice Consistently

Practice is often key to achieving excellence as it allows you to develop your skills and become more proficient at a task. To get the most out of your practice, it is important to be consistent and to set aside dedicated time to do it.

Seek Feedback and Be Open to Criticism

Seeking feedback and being open to criticism can help you identify areas where you need to improve and make adjustments to your approach. It is important to be open to constructive criticism and to use it as an opportunity to learn and grow.

Be Willing to Put in the Time and Effort

Achieving excellence often requires a willingness to put in the time and effort necessary to excel. This may involve making sacrifices or working hard to overcome challenges, but the effort can be worth it in the end.

Ultimately, achieving excellence requires dedication, hard work, and a willingness to continually learn and improve. It is a journey that may involve setbacks and challenges, but with perseverance and determination, you can achieve excellence in your chosen field.

REAP & ENJOY EXCELLENCE

Excellence always yields results. A lot of people may not be able to practice it, but many people appreciate it. Excellence attracts everything knowledge, understanding, skills, and wisdom attract. It puts you in a class of your own.

Ruth exemplified a life of excellence, which attracted Boaz to her, and opened doors of favor toward her. Look at what Boaz said: "Now, my daughter, do not be afraid. I will do for you whatever you ask, since all my people in the city know that you are a woman of excellence" (Ruth 3:11 AMP).

There are many rewards for excellence depending on your stream of effort. One ultimate reward is that God will be glorified through you and the works of your hand. This is likely what God will say, "Well done, good and faithful servant. You have been faithful and trustworthy over a little, I will put you in charge of many things; share in the joy of your master" (Matthew 25:23 AMP).

Other rewards to note include:

- Personal satisfaction: achieving excellence can bring a sense of personal accomplishment and pride.
- Recognition: excellence often leads to recognition from others such as awards, promotions, and other forms of public acknowledgment.
- Increased opportunities: excelling in your field can open up new opportunities for advancement and growth.
- Improved performance: a focus on excellence can lead to improved performance, which can result in better results and outcomes.

- Greater impact: excellence can lead to a greater ability to make a positive impact in your field or the world.
- Increased confidence: achieving excellence can boost self-confidence and self-esteem.
- Improved relationships: being known for excellence can lead to stronger relationships with colleagues, clients, and others.
- Financial rewards: in some fields, excellence can lead to financial rewards such as raises, bonuses, and other forms of compensation.

START AGAIN

Just as we stated at the beginning of this chapter, do not stop trying to excel. Your level of excellence last year might be mediocre in two years. The life of excellence is linear with the endpoint of death. So, at the point where you received a reward for excellence, the next question you should ask yourself is where you can start again. Never settle for less. Someone said, "Those who settle are always at the bottom."

CHAPTER FOUR

FOLLOW YOUR TIME ZONE

"Do not compare your progress with that of others. We all need our own time to travel our own distance."
—GERALD JAMPOLSKY

Time zones are very useful in the western world. This is one of the amazing things I got to experience when I migrated to the United States of America. It amazes me that I could be traveling from one time zone to another time zone in the same country. There are different time zones in the United States because the country is so large that it stretches across several degrees of longitude. When it is noon in one part of the country, it is not noon in all parts because the sun is at a different point in the sky at various times of the day. To avoid confusion, some parts of the country observe different times, and these differences are reflected in the time zones.

I once heard this story of a pastor who had to travel to another state for a conference to speak. He did not take notice of the different time zones. On his way, there was a great storm, and he had to slow down, stop, and maneuver his way through it. He thought he was very late for the meeting and he felt extremely bad. I'm sure he didn't have a device to update automatically when there is a change in the time zone. When he arrived at his destination, he quickly apologized to the organizer for being late. But the organizer said, "No, you are not late; we haven't even started. Have you forgotten we are operating in another time zone?"

Sometimes we worry so much that time is running out and we are not achieving our personal goals. We forget so easily that God operates in different time zones for different people. Comparing ourselves to others only robs us of our joy and peace. We are all on different paths, in different stages of life. We are all given different gifts, talents, and abilities. We are all unique and special in our way. "Embrace who you are and your journey."[1]—Brendon Burchard

> "Comparing ourselves to others only robs us of our joy and peace."

After high school, I had a little group where we searched for schools in the United States and looked up the requirements needed to gain admission. We didn't have access to Wi-Fi as we do now, so some nights, we all gathered in an office owned by one of the group member's mothers who was a lecturer at one of the universities. After some years, two of them got admission and left for the United States, while I stayed back in my country to go through medical school. After about twelve years, I had the opportunity to travel to the United States for my master's degree. At this point, my two friends who had gone before me had finished their undergraduate and master's and were working in prestigious companies. Of course, there was the pressure of feeling I was late on my career journey. But as I continued in my journey, God made me know I was just on time. I didn't lose time; I was just on my pathway to my destiny. Someone said, "The only person you should try to be better than is the person you were yesterday, and you don't compare yourselves with someone else's middle."

In 2 Corinthians 10:12, Paul writes, "We do not dare to classify or compare ourselves with some who commend themselves. When they measure themselves by themselves and compare themselves with themselves, they are not wise." This passage warns against the dangers of comparing ourselves to others and, instead, encourages us to focus on living up to our potential.

GOD'S TIMING

These two words seem contradictory when put together. Because God existed before time began and exists out of time. God cannot be controlled or confined by time. However, because man plans with time, we always love to explain God's actions by time, and so, we believe that God times the plan. We can only explain the actions of God by time so it can make sense to us. But in a real sense, God does what He does when He decides to do it for our good. For every believer, there is a plan or program designed by God. God has an assignment (that leads to a destiny) for every man. David said it this way; "My times are in your hand" (Psalm 31:15 KJV). Our responsibility is to follow God who has the plan, at his pace, until we reach the desired destination. Many times, God shows us the end at the beginning, and then takes us through a process that equips, enriches, enlightens, and empowers us for the destination.

> "However, because man plans with time, we always love to explain God's actions by time, and so, we believe that God times the plan."

Habakkuk, one of the minor prophets, realized that one of the problems of man is impatience. He wrote through the inspiration of the Holy Spirit saying, "For the vision is yet for the appointed [future] time It hurries toward the goal [of fulfillment]; it will not fail. Even though it delays, wait [patiently] for it, Because it will certainly come; it will not delay" (Habakkuk 2:3 KJV).

Impatience can be caused by internal desperation or

external pressure from people around. But if we learn to wait on God, we will receive what He has promised us.

One area where many young people are desperate and impatient is marriage. I have spoken to a lot of people, who due to pressure from time, family, and expectations, have opted to do anything to get married. Many have gotten into very toxic relationships because of this impatience. In the book of Exodus, the Israelites became impatient while waiting for Moses to return from Mount Sinai with the Ten Commandments. They asked Aaron to make a golden calf for them to worship, and Aaron complied, leading to the Israelites committing a great sin. Many times, we make counterfeits because we are not able to patiently wait for the original plan that God has for us. David said, "I waited patiently for the Lord; he turned to me and heard my cry" (Psalm 40:1 KJV).

Most times, impatience leads to bad decision-making and ultimate failure. Here are a few examples: Napoleon Bonaparte was a French statesman and military leader who is considered one of the greatest commanders in history. However, he was also known for his impatience and his tendency to make hasty decisions. One example of this is his decision to invade Russia in 1812, which ended in disaster and contributed to his downfall.

Julius Caesar was a Roman general and statesman who is considered one of the greatest military leaders in history.

However, he was also known for his ambition and his tendency to be impatient. This is exemplified by his decision to cross the Rubicon, a river in Italy, with his army in 49 BC, which marked the start of a civil war and ultimately led to his assassination.

Adolf Hitler was the leader of Nazi Germany and is widely considered one of the worst dictators in history. He is known for his impatience and his tendency to make rash decisions, such as his decision to invade the Soviet Union in 1941, which was a major turning point in World War II.

Bill Gates is a co-founder of Microsoft and is one of the wealthiest and most influential people in the world. However, he has admitted to making mistakes due to impatience, including the decision to launch Windows Vista before it was ready, which led to widespread criticism and customer frustration.

The Chinese Bamboo Tree gets to ninety feet in five weeks. Isn't that amazing and appealing? Imagine the speed of growth. The only other fact is that it takes five years after planting to do so. It requires daily nurturing, watering, and fertilizing, though there is not a single sprout. The result is beautiful, but the process requires patience, consistency, and discipline. One more thing, the farmer knows what he planted and where he planted it. Make sure you know what you're planting, and where you are planting it. If God is in it, it will surely sprout, and yes, expect speed.

COMPARISON

People often compare themselves to others as a way of evaluating their abilities, characteristics, and circumstances. This can be a natural and normal part of human psychology and can serve as a way for individuals to set goals, motivate themselves, and measure their progress. However, comparison can also lead to negative emotions such as jealousy, envy, and low self-esteem if it is not approached healthily. It's important to remember that everyone is unique and has strengths, weaknesses, and circumstances, and it is not productive or healthy to constantly compare oneself to others.

An eagle will be very frustrated if he tries to behave like a lion. They are both strong but operate in different ways. Avoid comparing your pathway and assignment with another person. It robs you of your uniqueness and limits you from achieving your purpose in life. "Pay careful attention to your work, for then you will get the satisfaction of a job well done, and you won't need to compare yourself to anyone else. For we are each responsible for our own conduct" (Galatians 6:4-5 NLT).

In another version, "Make a careful exploration of who you are and the work you have been given, and then sink yourself into that. Don't be impressed with yourself. Don't compare yourself with others. Each of you must take responsibility for doing the creative best you can with your own life" (Galatians 6:4-5 MSG).

Within one year after I arrived in the United States, I got married to my beloved wife. Now, this is what many of my distant friends heard, and they were surprised at how I did it. Well, many people who didn't bother to call and ask how it happened, took off from the first sentence and concluded I made some sharp moves to find a woman immediately after I got into America. Perhaps, because it is not uncommon for people to rally to marry American citizens to settle quickly. Well, those who called me knew the full story. I am sure you would like to know too. I courted my wife for about four years, three years before I traveled to America. Surprising to many, she was not a citizen at that time. I was not looking for a quick way out. She was chosen by God to follow me on my journey to our destination in life. Many people who did not know this full story compared their lives to mine, and unfortunately, they ended badly. I remember a friend of mine, who was also in the United States, came to meet me and said, "Victor, you got married so fast, and I would like to be like you." I said, "Please don't try to copy blindly. If you want to be like me, then you will have to go through everything I went through." Unfortunately, he rushed into marriage, and it has not been a nice story. Be careful not to compare yourself blindly with anyone.

J. K. Rowling, the author of the Harry Potter series, said that she struggled with feelings of inadequacy

> "Be careful not to compare yourself blindly with anyone."

and self-doubt early in her career and that comparing herself to other writers only made these feelings worse. She eventually learned to focus on her own goals and achievements rather than comparing herself to others.

CURE FOR COMPARISON

Several strategies can help you avoid unhealthy comparisons and maintain a healthy perspective:

Practice gratitude: focusing on the things you are grateful for can help you feel more content and less likely to compare yourself to others.

Remember that social media is not reality: it's important to remember that what people post online is often a carefully curated and filtered version of their lives, and it may not accurately represent their actual experiences or circumstances. I remember when I got married. My wife and I started our master's degree one week after we got married. We had to do a lot of long-distance communication because we were in separate states. She was at Carnegie Mellon University in Pennsylvania, while I was in a little town in Georgia called Statesboro where you had Georgia Southern University. A few months after we got married, we had to attend a friend's wedding in Florida. We were both living strictly on a budget because we only depended on our Graduate Assistantship pay, which was very little to allow for any extracurricular activity. I couldn't book a hotel for the wedding—I didn't even remember. There are many things you don't remember when you don't have the funds.

My wife joined me in Atlanta, and we boarded a bus with a family to Florida. Well, there were no rooms booked for us, and we didn't have the money to book on-site. So, we asked to squeeze in with the family. I remember not getting any bed space to lay my head. I had to stay on the floor of the room, not even on the couch. The next morning, we woke up, dressed up, headed to the venue, took some nice pictures, and I posted one or two on my Facebook page. That picture got so many likes, and I received several messages from people asking for financial help. Financial help? If only they knew they might have been even richer than me at that time. The picture deceived them—I think. Be careful of those you copy on social media. Don't make crucial decisions based on what you see on a profile.

Focus on your journey: rather than comparing yourself to others, try to focus on your own goals and progress. This can help you feel more fulfilled and motivated. I will discuss more about this in the next chapter.

Seek support: surrounding yourself with supportive friends and loved ones can help you feel more confident and less likely to compare yourself to others. Having the right people around you will motivate you, instead of making you feel insecure or inferior. One of my frequent prayers is that God will connect me with the right people. And yes, He surely does. God also connects you to the right people to sharpen your dreams and expose you to the level of excellence you need to compare yourself to.

Practice self-compassion: treating yourself with kindness and understanding, rather than harsh judgment can help you feel more positive about who you are and less inclined to compare yourself to others. If you are like me who does a lot of critical analysis of yourself, then you must be careful not to emphasize your weaknesses and downplay your strengths. Yes, have objectives and goals to achieve in life, but also be flexible with yourself. Don't accommodate laziness but give time for the process to work too.

Remember that it's natural to compare yourself to others from time to time, but it's important to approach comparison healthily and focus on your growth and development.

FOLLOW GOD

One thing that helps us to avoid comparison is knowing what God has destined for us. Many people are distracted by other people's pathways because they are not sure of what God has said concerning them. Jesus, at a time in His earthly ministry, went to the temple on the Sabbath Day as He always did. There, He did something very important: "He opened (unrolled) the book and found the place where it was written" (Luke 4:17 AMP). Jesus knew exactly what He came to do and would not compare Himself to any other man in any sense. All He had to do was obey and follow God all the way, despite what was happening around Him.

As a believer, it is always important to know what God is saying concerning you at every phase. If not, you will be at the mercy of others' sincere counsel and advice—probably coming from a source of human love but not God. You must always ask God for direction at every phase of your life, and what He wants you to do next, even if it does not align with the popular choice. The popular pathway for doctors who migrated to the United States is to go through the board exams, residency, and then practice. But I didn't go that route. At this moment, I can boldly say God led me to do otherwise.

> "You must always ask God for direction at every phase of your life, and what He wants you to do next, even if it does not align with the popular choice."

Being a medical doctor in the United States is very lucrative, so to many people, it looked as if I was going a dangerous route. I could not tell my story while I was going through this other process because it looked scary and strange. But at the end of that phase of my life, I was so joyous that I followed God's plan. It baffles me when many believers claim to know God but do not care to follow Him in simple things concerning their lives. When I served as a youth pastor, I interacted with many parents, especially when it came to choosing a career path for their children. It amazed me that many of them did not include God in making a choice. They preferred to rank their choices by job availability, lucrativeness, personal affinity, and similar mundane things. I am not insinuating that these things are unimportant, but I believe God is the Alpha and Omega. He is the beginning and the end. He knows the end from the beginning. Seasons change. Economies change. Inventions change. Whoever thought there would be a YouTube website where you can watch all types of videos for free or a time where you could order food from an app on your phone, and have it delivered to you at your home. The jobs that look lucrative today may not be in many years to come. Many jobs are being replaced by robots and artificial intelligence. Who knows what the world will be like in 20 years? Men can predict, but God certainly knows. Daniel saw many kings, regimes, cabinets, board meetings, and board directors, and he survived, not because he was smart, but because he was always in tune with God. God gave him wisdom and intelligence that carried him through the years, despite the attacks and persecutions.

RESTORATION OF TIME

Someone said the unit of destiny is time. And there is one thing I know about God; He is never late. God

"God always shows up when it matters, and if He does not show up, then it doesn't matter."

always shows up when it matters, and if He does not show up, then it doesn't matter. Yes, that sounds tough. But if God does not show up, then He has a better plan. God never fails to show up at the right time. You may ask, why did God wait until the three Hebrew children were thrown into the fire? Why did Jesus wait until Lazarus was in the grave for four days? Why did God not divide the Red Sea before Israel got there? There are many questions we may ask, but I am very sure that God is never late. I want to encourage you. After reading this chapter, you may wonder why your situation is different. Yes, you shouldn't compare yourself with others, but why does it look like God is not showing up for you? I just want you to know that God has never left you. He cannot forsake and forget you. He will surely show when it matters. And if you have lost anything in the space of waiting for God, He will restore everything and more to you. You cannot wait in vain. God said, "And I will restore to you the years that the locust hath eaten" (Joel 2:25 KJV).

CHAPTER FIVE
FOCUS ON YOUR FOCUS

"Concentrate all your thoughts upon the work at hand. The sun's rays do not burn until brought to a focus."
—ALEXANDER GRAHAM BELL

Focus refers to the ability to direct one's attention and mental energy toward a specific task or goal. It is the mental state of selectively being engaged and aware of present tasks and the ability to suppress distractions and irrelevant information. When you can maintain focus, you can work more efficiently and effectively toward achieving your goals. It is an important cognitive function that plays a key role in many aspects of life, from work and study to personal relationships and leisure activities. Every day in our lives, we are faced with numerous tasks, originating from us, or thrown at us by others. Your ability to focus in such cases depends on your capability to know what your priorities are.

Stephen Covey said, "The key is not to prioritize what's on your schedule but to schedule your priorities."[1]

This means we must first focus on our priorities and probably not even have time for things that do not align with our purpose. The success of any project or enterprise depends on the ability to stay focused, to stay on course, to stay committed. Over the years, I have seen the power of focus, determination, and consistency in the lives of people who have demonstrated excellence in all they do. I remember in one of the conferences I mentioned this. Someone asked a question. She asked why one cannot diversify into many things, especially in something like business. I answered that your diversification should lead to one purpose in life. Sometimes, trying to be everywhere puts you nowhere. Busyness does not always equal business. Lee Iacocca said, "The ability to concentrate and to use time well is everything."[2]

Apostle Paul was one man who practiced living a laser-focused life. He had a heavenly goal and that was his entire focus. Read some of his words in the Bible: I'm not saying that I have this all together, that I have it made. But I am well on my way, reaching out for Christ, who has so wondrously reached out for me. Friends don't get me wrong: By no means do I count myself an expert in all of this, but I've got my eye on the goal, where God is beckoning us onward—to Jesus. I'm off and running, and I'm not turning back. So, let's keep focused on that goal, those of us who want everything

God has for us. If any of you have something else in mind, something less than total commitment, God will clear your blurred vision—you'll see it yet! Now that we're on the right track, let's stay on it. (Philippians 3:13-15 MSG) In the Bible and contemporary times, there are numerous examples of people who focused on what they did until they became the focus of the world. There is a popular saying: "Focus on your focus so that one day you will be the focus."

Nehemiah was the king's cupbearer and when he heard that the walls of Jerusalem were in ruin, he developed a plan to build them. He rallied the people, secured permission and resources from the king, and managed to rebuild the wall in fifty-two days. This was not without a lot of distractions. Many times, people who didn't want him to succeed in rebuilding the wall spoke to him harshly and even plotted to kill him. But his focus and determination in the face of opposition led to the reconstruction of the walls of Jerusalem.

One of the greatest basketball players of all time, Michael Jordan, was known for his intense focus and dedication to the game. He spent countless hours practicing and perfecting his skills, which helped him to win six NBA championships and numerous individual awards throughout his career. Similar to Michael is Christian Ronaldo, who is arguably one of the greatest footballers (soccer) in history. He is known to be a very focused person and has a very disciplined routine.

Despite his exposure to wealth, fame, and criticism, he worked hard to remain valuable for many years in the game.

Albert Einstein's contributions to science were driven by his focus and dedication to understanding the nature of the universe. Despite facing many obstacles and setbacks, he remained determined in his work and made groundbreaking discoveries that changed the way we think about physics. Steve Jobs is known for his laser-like focus on design and user experience, which helped make Apple one of the most successful and innovative companies in the world. Despite many setbacks and personal health issues, he remained determined to bring his vision for Apple to life. Martin Luther King Jr. was an American Baptist minister and activist who focused on fighting for the rights of African Americans through nonviolent civil disobedience. Despite facing opposition and violence, he remained determined in his mission and his focus on achieving equality and civil rights for African Americans played a key role in the Civil Rights Movement. There are many more examples of those who demonstrated laser-like focus in their endeavors and made history in the world.

DISTRACTIONS

One thing you should know is that the Devil cannot destroy you (as a child of God) but he can

> "One thing you should know is that the Devil cannot destroy you (as a child of God) but he can distract you."

distract you. He knows if he can distract you, then you cannot achieve the plan you have, and even if you do, not at the time you should. There are three distractions I will discuss here, but I believe there could be more.

Fear

Fear is the reaction to a picture of a negative outcome that has or will never occur. It is a consequence of imagining a false reality. Fear is False Experiences Appearing Real. Fear is not always bad. There is an instinctive fear that protects us from danger. But that is not what we are discussing here. Here, I am referring to the fear that torments, the fear that distracts you from achieving what God has placed in your mind. Paul warned Timothy about this when he said, "For God has not given us a spirit of fear, but of power and of love and of a sound mind." (II Timothy 1:7 NKJV)

I remember my final year in medical school. It is common for our exams to include an oral discussion, where a panel of professors is formed to test each candidate verbally. I confess it was never fun. One of my colleagues, just before he entered the room where the panel members were seated, got very anxious. You could see the fear written all over him; he was sweating profusely. And when he got in to take his exams, he could not even remember his name. The fear was so much that he couldn't utter a word; instead, he was jittering and sweating. Although that was so strange to all of us, it illustrates what the spirit of fear can do to a person.

Peter and the other disciples had sailed on a boat leaving Jesus behind. But while they were in the middle of the sea, they saw someone walking on the water. This brought fear to all of them. In a bid to make sure they were not seeing a ghost, Peter asked Jesus to let him walk on water, so he could attest that He was Jesus. Jesus told him to step into the water. And amazingly, Peter stepped on the water and began to walk on it, just as Jesus did. He was full of faith in the words of Jesus until he began to look at the wind, the water, and the waves. Then, he imagined what would happen if he sank. Fear crippled his faith, and he began to sink. Thank God, Jesus reached out to him quickly (which was another miracle) to rescue him. Fear sinks us in the water of life and hinders us from focusing on the great things God has designed and planned for our lives.

Flesh

The flesh refers to the natural make-up, inner cravings, and normal proclivities of an individual. These things manifest in the form of habits or an extreme form: addictions and will usually bring us pleasure. We are often tempted by the things we love to do. Unfortunately, I have seen a young man who lost many opportunities and could not focus on what he had to do because he was distracted by an online computer game. He is a brilliant chap who confessed to this distraction when he disappointed himself and his family. He fell very short of what was expected in his academic results. Many people would have become great if not for the distraction of pleasure. Ernest Hemingway was a highly successful author and journalist, known for his spare, direct writing style and his experiences as a war correspondent. However, he could not get over the distraction of alcohol. He struggled with alcoholism throughout his life, which is believed to have contributed to his physical and mental decline. Hemingway's heavy drinking is said to have affected his ability to write and may have contributed to his suicide at the age of 61.

Samson was a great man. He was ordained to be a Nazarite before he was born. His name was given, and he was anointed to deliver the children of Israel from the Philistines who had disturbed them for a long time. Samson was endowed with special physical qualities that no one at that time could match or explain. He did extraordinary things: killing 1000 men with a jawbone of a donkey and lifting the city gates of Gaza that weighed about 4 tons (8000 pounds). However, one of his distractions was women. He escaped from many distractions until he had no more chances. One day, his secret leaked after the persuasion of a woman—Delilah—and he fell into the arms of the Philistines as a most wanted prisoner.

Solomon was also someone who got distracted by his affinity with women from foreign countries. He was later distracted from serving the true God and made way for various forms of idols to be worshiped during his reign. Never allow pleasure to take over your purpose. Say like Isaiah, "Because the Sovereign Lord helps me, I will not be disgraced. Therefore, I have set my face like a stone, determined to do his will. And I know that I will not be put to shame." (Isaiah 50:7 NLT).

Failure

Failure is coming short of your goal and objectives. One is said to have a failure when one does not reach the set mark either designed by an individual or by a system. Different systems have different measures of success. Many schools would have 50 percent as the passing mark for any subject, while others might have 60/70 percent. So, the expected success varies between systems and subjects. But failure is generally falling short of the mark you have set for yourself or set by the system. One of the major failures of my life that got me was in medical school. Before then, I had never cried for failing an exam, but this time, I wept as a baby would. I remember calling my immediate elder brother to tell him I had failed, and I cried so badly. I had put so much effort into it: reading all night, getting various materials, attending lectures and study groups, and so many investments. So, when I was told I failed, I wept bitterly. The shame was compounded by the fact that I had just preached a message to the college fellowship of my church then. It was a message that encouraged all students to excel and go beyond their obstacles. The topic of that sermon was "The Spirit that Conquers," which became the title of my first book. After that failure, God reminded me to go back to the sermon I had preached. The outline was my comfort through the period of my preparation for the second attempt at the professional exam.

Failure is always a part of everyone's success story. It is not the end of the world. Don't ever let failure stop you from focusing on the bright future God has for you. We do not always see the failures of great men because we only see them when they are great. If you would let them tell you their stories, then you would understand the glory behind their success. Unfortunately, Judas Iscariot failed himself, his friends (other disciples), and Jesus. But that was not the end of the game. If only he had waited to see the resurrected Jesus. Sadly, he committed suicide before he had the opportunity to be forgiven and start on a new slate. Failure, especially in a major aspect of life such as a career, financial stability, or personal relationships, can lead to feelings of hopelessness,

> "Don't ever let failure stop you from focusing on the bright future God has for you."

helplessness, and depression. These feelings can escalate to a point where people may feel that suicide is the only solution to their problems. Aaron Swartz, a computer programmer, entrepreneur, and internet activist who was involved in several high-profile projects, including the development of the RSS web feed format and the creation of the social news website (Reddit) was arrested on federal charges related to the alleged unauthorized downloading of academic articles from the JSTOR online database. Despite his efforts to fight the charges, he faced the possibility of a long prison sentence and a costly legal battle. Unfortunately, though many other factors might have contributed, he committed suicide in 2013 at the age of 26.

Failure is never the end of a story; it is just a part of the story. You should not hinder yourself from tomorrow's opportunities because of yesterday's failures. Never give suicide and depression the opportunity to deprive you of tomorrow's beauty. Every day is a new day. It reminds me of this song by Jeff and Sheri Easter[3]:

> *Every day is a new day*
> *Every dawn is a new sunrise*
> *Every beauty He placed here for me*
> *Every day is a new day*
> *Every journey He's by my side*
> *And never will I see this world the same*

FOCUS ENHANCERS

Determination

Determination is the force behind focus when faced with challenges along the journey. Determination is the quality of being resolute; the act of deciding firmly on a course of action. It is the act of reaching a decision and then continuing to work toward achieving a goal. It is also the act of being persistent in pursuing a goal despite any obstacles or setbacks. It is difficult to focus on your journey when faced with challenges. Determination kept me going in my medical school journey. It is rare to find a medical student who did not at one point in time face challenges along the way. For me, it was not just the voluminous curriculum, but also the ridicule, mockery, embarrassment, complex issues, and many other challenges I faced in the process. I recall one of those days, as a student, we were doing a pediatric ward round. The resident doctor who was leading us picked on me and asked me the three signs of heart failure to watch out for in children. Well, I knew the answer but pronounced the word wrong. The word was "Tachycardia," but I pronounced it "Tachicardia" with a stress on the "ch" letters. She busted into laughter, made a mockery of my pronunciation many times, and even called me that in place of my name throughout the ward round. That was the height of embarrassment for me, but I would not let it hinder me from reaching my end goal.

Determination is the force behind focus. What will you say of Nelson Mandela, who spent 27 years in prison for his fight against apartheid in South Africa, but never gave up on his goal of ending racial segregation and promoting equality? A few weeks after I found out that I would not be able to pay for my school fees and accommodation, my guardian called me out to his sitting room. He asked me a very important question in the presence of his wife. He asked, "How much do you have?" I said, "I have $400." He was dumbfounded. How could I survive with $400? It could not even get me a room for one month in the city of Atlanta. When he told me to go back into my room, he said something to his wife without knowing I had heard. He said, "Victor is determined. Let's see how we can help him." They saw the determination in my eyes.

Discipline

Discipline is the act of training and developing oneself to abide by routines and habits that enhance focus and success. It is the ability to control one's behavior, emotions, and desires to achieve a goal. Discipline might require you to set goals. Having clear, measurable goals can help you stay focused on what you want to achieve and avoid getting sidetracked. Discipline also allows you to prioritize your tasks, so you can focus on the most important ones first and avoid wasting time on less important tasks. Discipline enables you to eliminate distractions like social media or unnecessary notifications so that you can focus on your work without interruptions. Discipline helps you manage your time more efficiently, allowing you to focus on one task at a time, instead of multitasking and getting overwhelmed. Discipline helps you develop self-control, which is key to staying focused. It allows you to resist temptations and distractions and stay on track toward your goals. Ultimately, discipline is essential for maintaining focus, and it takes time and practice to develop this skill.

There are countless stories of people who, unfortunately, lost track of their purpose because they were not disciplined. This was the story of someone I knew some time ago. He was such an intelligent person, a great consultant in his field, very jovial, and carried a presence everyone loved. He was also a very good, devoted Christian until he got distracted by women. He started flirting with one, then two, then more, and everything began to dwindle. He later got married, but his marriage did not last for too long, despite having a child. He abandoned his wife and child, went to another place, and his life has not changed. Sometimes, I wondered how his life would have been if he had been disciplined. His downfall was women and sex, but for others, it is money, games, fame, and bad friends.

Diligence

Diligence is being hardworking, persistent, and attentive to detail. It is the willingness to put in a steady effort to achieve a goal or complete a task. Diligence is characterized by careful and conscientious work and a strong sense of purpose. It often involves working hard, paying attention to details, and being willing to put in extra time and effort to achieve a specific objective. Diligence is an important trait for success in many areas of life, from school and work to personal projects and hobbies. You might wonder what the difference between diligence and determination is. Diligence is more about the hard work and effort put in, while determination is more about the mindset and attitude toward the goal. Both are important and often go hand in hand as diligence is needed to put in the hard work, and determination is needed to stay focused and not give up on the goal. I know many determined people who are not diligent in what they do. They want to do what they do, but they are not ready to put in the work to succeed at it. John C. Maxwell said diligence

> "I know many determined people who are not diligent in what they do. They want to do what they do, but they are not ready to put in the work to succeed at it."

is the engine of success. "Seest thou a man diligent in his business? he shall stand before kings; he shall not stand before mean men" (Proverbs 22:29 KJV). Diligence is what often separates the person with distinction from the average.

There are numerous rewards for focus, and I will share some of them here:

Here are a few examples:

- Increased productivity: when you focus on a task, you are more likely to complete it in a shorter amount of time and with better-quality results. This increased productivity can lead to more success and recognition in your job or other endeavors.
- Improved decision-making: when you focus, you can process information more efficiently and make better decisions. This can lead to more successful outcomes in business and personal interactions.
- Greater creativity: when you focus, you allow yourself to enter a state of flow where your mind can explore new ideas and connect seemingly unrelated concepts. This can lead to greater creativity and problem-solving abilities.
- Better memory retention: when you focus, you are more likely to remember important information. This can be especially beneficial in academic or professional settings.

- Increased sense of satisfaction: when you focus on a task, you can immerse yourself in it and experience a sense of accomplishment and satisfaction when it is completed.
- Reducing stress: when you focus on one task at a time, you can reduce the feeling of being overwhelmed by multiple responsibilities. This can decrease stress levels and increase feelings of well-being.
- Better self-awareness: when you focus on your thoughts and emotions, you can gain a better understanding of yourself and your motivations. This can lead to greater self-awareness and the ability to make positive changes in your life.

CHAPTER SIX
FIRMLY MAKE DECISIONS

"We all make choices, but in the end, our choices make us."
—KEN LEVINE

We never stop making decisions in life. We make choices and will continue to do so every day. Though I believe it is never too late to make good decisions in life, it is very important to make good decisions at certain stages of your life to reap the best outcome. When you are not making good decisions, you are making bad decisions. Inaction is no decision but a decision not to act. Yes, all seasons of life are opportunities to make good decisions, but the impact of a good decision is based on the right season.

> **"When you are not making good decisions, you are making bad decisions."**

Soccer is one of my favorite games that I love to play and

watch. A typical match between two teams lasts for about ninety minutes, with probably 2-5 minutes added, depending on the events that occurred in the game. A good result (goal) is when a ball is placed into the opponent's net. In a typical game between two teams, there will be opportunities to score goals; sometimes the players take them, and, at other times, those opportunities are missed. A ball in the net within the minutes of play is called a goal and would count on the scoreboard. A ball in the net after the match is over is not counted as a goal, no matter who plays it. Because it was not played during the period of the match.

Life can be like this. There is a period in your life when some decisions are very crucial to make. Making those decisions after that period does not have the same impact as if you did during the right period. There was this boy who grew up in my neighborhood. He was reluctant to go the normal route every common child would go through. He dropped out of school very early and refused to go back. Due to that, he could not read and write. Then he joined gangs in the neighborhood to cause various riots and havoc. But he forgot that time does not pause for you to make the right decisions. Many years later, he still has not made the right choices. He got involved with various ladies and had some children, but still could not read or write, nor did he qualify for any job. In fact, he did not even want to work, but rather, he used the money he got from friends and family to gamble.

Years later, nothing good has come of it. He is living with the consequences of his past decisions, yet, not making the right decisions. This is a very pitiable state to be in.

There are many reasons why several good people do not make sound decisions, even when they are led by God to do so. One big factor is the lack of tenacity, confidence, and courage to make those decisions. Great people today are those who made great decisions despite great setbacks and challenges. I remember when I knew it was time to move to America. This was a dream I had kept for many years without fruition because I could not bring it to reality. Dreams do not become reality except timely decisions are made. Once I could take some steps to bring this into reality, I had to do so firmly and on time. Everything around me told me it was time. God used Bishop TD Jakes at that time to speak to me through his series on the Eagles and their babies. I knew it was time to leave my comfortable nest and step out to learn how to fly. It had to be a firm decision because some people were not happy with it. I had a good job in one of the private hospitals in the city where I lived. I was making some money that would keep me comfortable at least. So, those close to me felt I was making a mistake and trying to be over-ambitious. But I knew within me it was time to move. I did not have everything I needed to survive after moving, but I had

> "Dreams do not become reality except timely decisions are made."

everything I had to make the move. Many years later, people who did not understand what I was doing back then, now thank God for my decision at that time. One of my leaders who visited me recently said he thought I was too ambitious and making a hasty decision then, but now the results have shown it was the best decision I had made at that time.

VISION

One of the factors that help with making a good timely decision is having a vision. Vision is the ability to see God's purpose for your life in every phase. The vision you have should always be tied to your purpose. Your purpose is the end goal of your life; the Bible says your expected end. Jesus replied to Pilate after he was arrested and said, "Thou sayest that I am a king. To this end was I born, and for this cause came I into the world, that I should bear witness unto the truth. Everyone that is of the truth heareth my voice." (John 18:37 KIV)

Jesus knew what His end would look like. So, He walked and worked toward His end, His purpose in life. "Where there is no vision, the people perish" (Proverbs 29:18 KJV). The word "perish" here could be misleading as to the true meaning of what happens when there is no vision. Let's see other versions of that verse:

"Where there is no vision [no revelation of God and His

word], the people are unrestrained; But happy and blessed is he who keeps the law [of God]" (Proverbs 29:18 AMP).

"When there's no vision, the people get out of control, but whoever obeys instruction is happy" (Proverbs 29:18 CEB).

"If people can't see what God is doing, they stumble all over themselves; But when they attend to what he reveals, they are most blessed" (Proverbs 29:18 MSG).

"When people do not accept divine guidance, they run wild. But whoever obeys the law is joyful" (Proverbs 29:18 NLT)

It becomes very clear what the word "perish" means when we look at various versions. Let's summarize these thoughts using the word PERISH. So, where there is no vision, people are:

P – Poor in Knowledge: they do not know what they should know about themselves and do not even have any options to choose from. This reminds me of the first time I visited the Subway restaurant. I was just a few months into the United States, so it was so new to me. I was expecting to see a list of options (1 - 10), and then I would just randomly choose a number I thought would fit my taste. But then, to my amazement, I didn't see a ready-made option I could choose. I asked if I could get the same menu as the last person, but the servers could not understand. I asked the person behind me if he could help, and he also seemed confused. Then, I knew I was in a real situation. Anyways, I managed to get something out of that restaurant. Well since then I have learned the menu. If you don't know what to choose from, then you are liable to make the wrong choice. This is why we need God to enlighten our eyes to see His plans for us.

E – Experimental: people who lack vision take on anything and everything. They follow everyone's advice, even if they do not understand. They use their lives like an experiment. They are not sure if the experiment will succeed or fail. There is no plan for the choice of courses to study in college; they only choose them because a friend says they are good courses. They venture into business without due diligence because they see the advert on TV.

R – Resistant to Change: they prefer to remain in their comfort zones. People without vision are always comfortable with mediocrity. You will not be able to go to the next phase of your life when there is no vision. You are liable to remain stuck in one position because of comfort. I remember when I had to do compulsory volunteer work in a village in Nigeria. I had already planned during my stay there; I would write my exams and get my documents ready to move to the next stage of my life. But then, after that year, the pastor there did not want me to leave. He promised everything that would encourage a young adult like me to be comfortable. This was a good gesture. The only issue was that it did not align with the vision of my life. Sadly, I had to part ways with him after

I was done there. When you have a vision, you are not scared to make a change when it is time to do so.

I – Indecisive: unfortunately, I see many young people who find it very difficult to make decisions because they do not have any plans or visions for their lives. Having a vision helps you to make timely decisions.

S – Slack: when there is no vision, people are not motivated to do anything. There is no push to move forward. I also see many young people in this state. They are not motivated to go to the next phase of their lives. They settle into a place, and, of course, after some time, they settle at the bottom.

H – Hindrance to others' progress: one of the biggest challenges of a leader is trying to progress while surrounded by other leaders who do not have a vision. It is very difficult. I have worked in a group where I wrote down the vision and mission, goals and objectives, plans, and proposals to move the body forward. But because the other people I worked with did not seem to have any vision, everything was aborted. I could only do as much as they allowed me to do. It was a tough situation.

MIND

The mind is the power of man. Vision is conceived and developed in the mind. The mind of a man is like the roar of a lion, the speed of a cheetah, the strength of a gorilla, or the teeth of a panther. What differentiates us from other animals is the capability of the mind. This is why man has the power to control other animals, despite not being the tallest, strongest, fastest, or loudest on planet Earth. The mind is so important to what we can become in life. It reflects the capacity at which we can receive from God. During a presentation recently, I tried to explain it this way. Imagine that God has one terabyte worth of information to give you, and He wants to deposit it into your mind. If your mind can only receive one megabyte, then you cannot receive all the information God has for you. It will take longer than expected to download, decode, delete, and re-download. Remember that the thoughts of God are higher than our thoughts like the heavens are higher than the earth. But then, God wants to deposit some of those thoughts in us, so we can be like Him in manifesting divine life. Can your mind receive what the Holy Spirit reveals to you? Eyes have not seen; ears have not heard, nor the heart imagine what God has prepared for His people. But His Spirit has revealed them to us, yes!

Having said that, it is one thing to have a revelation; it is another thing to receive that revelation. It takes a ready mind to receive what God has revealed to you because surely, it will not look like what you have seen before. There is nothing new under the earth, but new things always erupt from heaven.

"And be not conformed to this world: but be ye transformed by the renewing of your mind, that ye may prove what is that good, and acceptable, and perfect, will of God" (Romans 12:2). Paul emphasized in this verse that transformation comes through the renewing of the mind. Think of it like deleting files from a hard drive or formatting it, so you can make space and have access to receive more of what God has in store for you. This teaches that the power of the mind lies in the ability to renew it, to change our thoughts and beliefs to align them with God's will. The Devil knows this concept too, and he attacks our minds many times because he knows if he can target the mind, then he can target our destinies. Paul also told us that we should guard our minds against negative thoughts and influences. "Finally, brothers and sisters, whatever is true, whatever is noble, whatever is right, whatever is pure, whatever is lovely, whatever is admirable—if anything is excellent or praiseworthy—think about such things" (Philippians 4:8 NIV). We should focus our thoughts on positive, uplifting things to protect our minds from negative influences. One powerful tool that Paul teaches us is "Casting down arguments and every high thing that exalts itself against the knowledge of God, bringing every thought into captivity to the obedience of Christ" (2 Corinthians 10:5 NKJV).

According to many other studies, one of the key concepts that underlie the power of the mind in achieving our vision is the idea of self-efficacy. Self-efficacy is the belief in one's ability to accomplish a task or goal. Research has shown that individuals with high levels of self-efficacy are more likely to set challenging goals for themselves, persist in the face of obstacles, and ultimately achieve their goals. This is one reason why those who have low self-esteem find it difficult to live up to their purpose in life. I remember struggling with low-self-esteem twice in my lifetime. One was during my teenage years when I had a skin disease called eczema, which made me so shy and uncomfortable that I could not stand to do what I normally would. This was a very big struggle until some people came around me to walk me through that time.

The other, which was more impactful in my life, was during the 4th and 5th years of medical school. Though I was active in church, I did not believe in my ability to understand what was being taught during those times in college. And as expected, my grades were poor. My low self-esteem made me hide from the lecturer in class, and I would always dodge answering questions. I didn't even bother to think of an answer to any question thrown at me because I just had the mind that I did not know it. My answer was always "I don't know." This continued for about two years before I realized what was wrong with me. I knew I was not born a dullard. I got into medical school because I was intelligent. So, what happened? The first step in dealing with this was to trace my way back to when it started. What triggered it? Why was

I feeling the way I did at the time? What changed? Then I realized that it all started when I got a lower score than expected in my anatomy class in Year 2. I was a very active member of the class, especially in anatomy lab sessions. I led the group in finding arteries and muscles in cadavers. I enjoyed doing that so much and was so good at it many members of the class noticed and hailed me often. I went into the exam hall with that confidence, but to my amazement, I got a C grade on my anatomy paper. I was so disappointed. Then, I figured maybe I was not as good as I thought I was. This was when I started retracting inward until I had very low self-esteem. So, realizing this was my first step in getting back up.

Then I gradually changed my network of friends. I began to surround myself with people who knew they were good, and there was no need to apologize for it. During the end of my 5th and the beginning of my 6th year of college, my mentality began to change. I became bolder in class. I dared to give any question a try; if it was wrong then it is wrong. My self-esteem began to improve despite challenges and setbacks.

One day, I was given the privilege to preach at the Christian Medical Student Association meetings. It would be our last meeting as students before our final exams that would determine our fate as new doctors. I preached Psalm 23 and illustrated the need for God to lead us as we enter another phase of our lives. A few hours after I preached, I went back to studying with my new group of friends. Then I muttered some words of fear and discouragement while reading. One of my friends looked at me in surprise. He reminded me of what I had just taught them and wondered why I uttered those kinds of words. He asked if I believed what I taught them in the meeting. They believed all of it and expected that I, the person who preached the word, would believe it too. This was another turning point in my life. It changed my orientation and the way I looked at myself. My final exams were the best exams I wrote in college because I did them knowing who I was and who was backing me up to succeed—the Holy Spirit.

Another important concept is the role of mental imagery in achieving our vision. Mental imagery involves using our imagination to create vivid, detailed images of what we want to achieve. This can be done through visualization exercises, where individuals spend time, each day imagining themselves successfully achieving their goals. Research has shown that mental imagery can have a positive impact on motivation, self-confidence, and goal attainment. You must have the ability to see it before you can seize it. Remember when God told Abraham to visualize his blessings? He told Abraham to look into the sky and count the stars. God knew Abraham could not count the stars, but He wanted him to have mental imagery of the blessings He promised him. You should be able to visualize your vision. You should have a mental picture of the future you want to feature in.

Elisha followed Elijah for many miles because he wanted to get something. Elijah kept asking him to go back, but he continued following. Elisha said to Elijah that he wanted a double portion of his power. Elijah said something very important. He said it is a very hard thing, but "if thou see me." The sight was a precursor to receiving double power. If you know the end of the story, Elisha saw it when Elijah was taken, and he seized the mantle; that was it. According to records, he doubled the number of Elijah's miracles. If you have a vision, then have a visualization of it. Write or draw the plan somewhere.

> "You should have a mental picture of the future you want to feature in."

PRESSURE

It is common in life to feel pressure from different angles and sources. This is feeling compelled to do something in reaction to internal or external forces. Pressure can affect us positively or negatively, depending on how we handle and channel the force behind it.

- Personal Pressure: personal pressure comes from our goals and ambitions in life. Sometimes, we feel so pressured because we are not meeting the goals and dates, we have set for ourselves while working toward our vision. Other times, it is the pressure from failure. Failing exams, relationships, job assessments, and other parts of life can increase the pressure on us.

- Peer Pressure: pressure can come from our peers. Many people limit peer pressure to teens because it seems more noticeable at that age. But peer pressure never stops. I remember when I bought our home, I was constantly under pressure to make my grass greener than that of my neighbors. Pressure keeps coming in one form or the other.
- People Pressure: pressure can come from people: our relatives, friends, community groups, and even children. People, in their innocence and so much care for you, might put some pressure on you. They want you to get married at a certain age. Then, when you get married, they begin to ask for children after nine months. Then, after one child, they come to you for another child. It never stops.
- Purposeful Pressure: this is positive pressure that we should all focus on. We should not let other forms of pressure pull us down. But we should focus on the purpose of God for our lives.

"And we know that in all things God works for the good of those who love him, who[a] have been called according to his purpose" (Romans 8:28 NIV). The best way to channel your pressures toward purpose is by learning how to make firm decisions based on the vision God has given you. If you do not have a vision and dare to make firm decisions, you will be easily derailed by pressure. Many years ago, I arrived in the United States as a medical doctor, but before I came, God had already directed me on what to do. I honestly did not understand why God led me in a very different way from what most medical doctors would do. But it attracted a lot of comments and pressure from well-wishers, elders, friends, and relatives. It looked as if I had made the biggest mistake of my life. But what saved me was the ability to firmly make a decision and focus on the vision God had given me before I arrived in America. I was so happy it was clear what to do before I arrived.

> "The best way to channel your pressures toward purpose is by learning how to make firm decisions based on the vision God has given you."

The other aspect of pressure in my life was to get married to an American citizen, which would have saved me a lot of hard work. Again, thank God he showed me my wife before I arrived in the United States. She was not with me at that time. I could have opted to break the relationship and start another one here, which many people do. But by God's grace, I was pressured to purpose. God gave me my wife so we can achieve kingdom purpose.

CHAPTER SEVEN
FAITH IT

"Faith is the strength by which a shattered world shall emerge into the light."
—HELEN KELLER

My father-in-law looked into my wife's (fiancé then) eyes and asked her a very strong question. He asked, "How is he going to make it?" He was referring to me. I had just left for the shores of America with only about $500. Though I got promises of funds that would help me pay off my graduate school fees, there was no full guarantee they would come. I never got those promised funds. My wife answered, "He's going by faith." That sounded hilarious. I would not advise anyone to do what I did. It was a big risk. But faith involves taking risks—and yes, big ones. Why would you need faith if you could predict tomorrow? I am sure you have heard: "Fake it until you make it" but I love to say, "Faith it until you make it".

Actually, if you can faith it, then you can certainly make it.

There are many powerful words that the Bible did not define, but faith was not one of them. "Now faith is the assurance (title deed, confirmation) of things hoped for (divinely guaranteed), and the evidence of things not seen [the conviction of their reality—faith comprehends as fact what cannot be experienced by the physical senses]" (Hebrews 11:1 AMP).

Faith is a spiritual science. Science says, "Seeing is believing," while faith says, "Believing is seeing." I have always loved defining faith as the enzyme that catalyzes supernatural reactions. There are some moves you cannot make or sustain without having faith. You need strong faith to make big moves, and you need trusting faith to sustain those moves.

> "You need strong faith to make big moves, and you need trusting faith to sustain those moves."

ACTIVATE

One of my favorite verses when it comes to faith is found in 1 John 5:4. It says, "For everyone born of God is victorious and overcomes the world, and this is the victory that has conquered and overcomes the world—our [continuing, persistent] faith [in Jesus the Son of God]."

Our journey of faith starts once we give our lives to Jesus Christ. Our faith in Jesus Christ is what activates the faith we need to believe God's promises and navigate our journey in life. Without faith, it is impossible to please God.

Salvation comes through faith in Jesus Christ. Paul says, "If you confess with your mouth the Lord Jesus and believe in your heart that God has raised Him from the dead, you will be saved" (Romans 10:9 NKJV). Once you are saved, you receive faith to conquer the world and reach heights beyond human imagination. At salvation, we receive a measure of faith "as God has dealt to each one a measure of faith" (Romans 12:3 NKJV).

LEVELS

The Bible, especially in the New Testament, illustrates different levels of faith. Jesus described the faith of His disciples as "little faith" when they woke Him during the storm. They had just witnessed Jesus preaching the Sermon on the Mount, and, as they came down from the mountainside, they also witnessed Him perform many miracles. Jesus healed a man with leprosy, a centurion's servant just by speaking the word, and touched Peter's mother-in-law and her fever left her. That same evening, he went out and healed demon-possessed people and all the sick people who were brought to Him. After all this, the disciples still demonstrated fear during the storm. Jesus had to let them know they had little faith.

A similar level of faith is what I will call the "blowing faith." This faith looks big but has no root and depth such that during trials or temptations, it flushes away. Remember when Jesus walked on water and Peter asked to also walk on water? Peter got a faith rush. He had the faith to walk on the sea for some time, then when he saw the storm, everything flushed out like a balloon plucked by a pin. "And immediately Jesus stretched forth his hand, and caught him, and said unto him, O thou of little faith, wherefore didst thou doubt?" (Matthew 14:31 KJV).

Jesus also described a level of faith as "great faith." This adjective was used when the centurion and the Gentile woman from Cana requested that Jesus heal their son and daughter respectively. Jesus did not expect that level of faith from these strangers, especially since they had not been taught the fundamentals of the faith. Proximity to the source of teaching does not automatically mean you would have great faith.

The Bible also highlighted the strong faith of Abraham. It says, "He staggered not at the promise of God through unbelief; but was strong in faith, giving glory to God" (Romans 4:20 KJV). The question you might have was were there not times that Abraham and Sarah doubted? Of course, they were times, but Abraham continued to grow in faith. As Paul said when he thanked the Thessalonian Christians, our faith should not be stranded at one level but should grow exceedingly: "We are bound to thank God always for you, brethren, as it is fitting, because your faith grows

> "Our faith should not be stranded at one level but should grow exceedingly."

exceedingly, and the love of every one of you all abounds toward each other" (1 Thessalonians 1:3 NKJV). Abraham's faith when he had Isaac cannot be compared to his faith when he had to sacrifice Isaac. There is a level of faith that makes you obey God radically.

DEVELOP

Seeing we have various levels of faith; the question is how do we grow and develop our faith? There are several ways to do this.

- Meditation on the Word of God: "Faith comes by hearing, and hearing by the word of God" (Romans 10:17 NKJV). It is one thing to hear the Word of God using your ears; it is another thing to hear using your heart. When you have heard or read the Word of God, you must meditate on it until your heart hears it. Once your heart (your spirit) has received the Word, the effect

    > **"When you have heard or read the Word of God, you must meditate on it until your heart hears it."**

    of the Word emanates from your spirit to your soul and then to your body. I heard the testimony of a woman who was diagnosed with cancer. She refused to meditate on the medical reports; rather, she kept meditating on the promises of God for her life until every cancer cell in her body left. I also remember when we had an issue with getting our second child. We tried many times and failed. At one point, I just wanted to accept fate; maybe we were not ready for a second child. But my wife decided to listen and digest faith messages. By the time she was done, I saw her manifesting a higher level of faith until we conceived and by God's grace had our second child.

- Prayer: "Therefore I say to you, whatever things you ask when you pray, believe that you receive them, and you will have them" (Mark 11:24 NKJV). Prayer is the ladder that connects us to the blessings God already has for us. Many people wonder why we need to pray when we have the blessings already. Prayer is the bank to cash the cheque God already gave you. The check is useless just sitting on your table without cashing it. Our prayer should be accompanied by faith and specificity. The more you pray in faith, using the Word of God you have meditated upon, the more your faith increases. You begin to see the results.
- Confession: "Let the redeemed of the Lord say so, Whom He has redeemed from the hand of the enemy" (Psalm 107:2 NKJV). You must speak what you want into existence. Don't contradict your prayers with

your words. Remember. God created the earth by speaking what was already conceived in His mind. The creation hears. This is the reason Jesus said if you say to the mountain be thou removed, it shall be removed. He said to his disciples after he cursed the fig tree, and the tree dried up. Our confessions should not be mere words, but words emanating from the place of understanding the promises of God and having strong confidence in your prayers. This is the differentiating line between confession and motivation talks. For motivational speakers, they speak before believing, but for believers, we believe before we speak. We don't see the manifestation just because we spoke, but because we believe what we spoke.

- Obedience: "Jesus said to them, "Fill the waterpots with water." And they filled them up to the brim". Faith is obedience. Once you are doing everything listed in the aforementioned points, instructions will come from God to you. Your promptness to obey God's instructions is the secret to hastening your expectations. Obedience always comes with a blessing. The servants at the wedding Jesus attended did not know much about Him. But they were warned by Mary to do whatsoever Jesus told them to do. Mary knew the secret to miracles is obedience. Thank God they obeyed, and their obedience resulted in the first miracle Jesus performed.

- Thanksgiving: "Do not be anxious or worried about anything, but in everything [every circumstance and situation] by prayer and petition with thanksgiving, continue to make your [specific] requests known to God" (Philippians 4:6 AMP). Thanksgiving is an important ingredient of faith. It takes faith to be thankful and even though we have not received the answers, we believe God has answered and we thank Him for it. Thanksgiving should be the habit of every believer, and we should never get tired of it. We should never get to the point where we feel entitled to God's blessings and answers to our prayers. Our thanksgiving should not be based on events, the economy, or expectations but on God's enduring mercies. I remember one of those days when my younger daughter joined me while I was eating. After I gave her a little bite, she said "thank you". Then she asked for more, and after I gave her the second bite, she didn't say "thank you" again. She just wanted more. The first time, she was grateful, but the second time, she felt entitled. Often, we can become entitled to God's blessings and forget to be thankful. It's important to never stop expressing gratitude to God, even before receiving blessings.

- Patience: "That you do not become [a]sluggish but imitate those who through faith and patience inherit the promises" (Hebrews 6:12 NKJV). After prayer, you need the patience to allow the process to produce the answers from God. Waiting on God might seem hard, but it renews our strength and makes our faith stronger. The result of impatience has never been good. Impatience will make you settle for the counterfeit, while the original is on the way. Be patient.

If you have read this book to this point, congratulations! I believe you have learned one or two things that will align your decision-making with your purpose in life. Do not ignore the lessons you have learned in this book; do more research on the topics; create action plans and put everything into practice. I believe you will see a change in your life for the better. God will crown all your efforts with excellence, guide you with grace, and make your life glorify His name. In Jesus' name. Amen!

DISCUSSION QUESTIONS

Chapter 1

1. The author suggests that many people may be religious but not "regenerated," meaning that they have not experienced a true spiritual transformation. What does it mean to be "born again," and how does this concept relate to the broader idea of salvation in Christianity?
2. Do you believe that finding God is a personal journey, or can it be influenced by external factors? (Finding God)
3. Have you ever had a personal experience that strengthened your faith or made you question it? (Finding God)
4. What are some of the distractions that may prevent people from fulfilling their ultimate purpose on earth? How can one overcome such distractions? (Seeking God)

5. How can a person who is struggling with addiction find deliverance, and what role can accountability partners play in the process? (Seeking God)
6. How can young adults maintain their spiritual lives while navigating through a world full of temptations and triggers? What strategies and tools can be used to create an environment for purity in all aspects of life? (Live Scenario)
7. The discussion highlights the importance of having an accountability partner to help young adults struggling with lust and pornography. What role can the church play in creating a safe space for individuals to share their struggles and receive support without fear of judgment or condemnation? (Live Scenario)
8. How can a person discern what God's purpose is for their life? What steps can one take to ensure they are on the right path and fulfilling their purpose? (Fulfilling Purpose)
9. In a society that often equates success with money and fame, how can individuals prioritize finding fulfillment and purpose over financial gain? How can we shift our mindset to focus on God's plan and purpose for our lives rather than the world's definition of success? (Fulfilling Purpose)

Chapter 2

1. Have you ever had a dream that you desired so much that it fueled your actions and ultimately led to its actualization? How did your desire for the dream affect your attitude towards it? (Desire your dreams)
2. How can someone tell the difference between a dream that is from God and one that is just a normal human desire or fantasy? Are there any specific signs or characteristics to look out for? (Desire your dreams)
3. Can desires change over time, and if so, what happens to the dreams associated with those desires? Is it possible to still actualize a dream that was once desired but no longer is? (Desire your dreams)
4. What are some practical steps one can take to feed and nurture a dream or vision planted by God? (Feed your dreams)
5. How can exposure to different skills and experiences help us in fulfilling our God-given dreams and aspirations? (Feed your dreams)
6. How can you stay motivated and persistent in pursuing your dreams, even when faced with challenges and setbacks? (Feed your dreams)
7. How can we overcome the fear of adapting to God's plans when it requires leaving our comfort zones? (Fish Big)

8. Can you think of a time when you had a big idea but did not pursue it because it seemed too daunting? What could you have done differently in hindsight? (Fish Big)
9. In what ways can we ensure that we are open to receiving and recognizing big ideas and opportunities from God? (Fish Big)
10. Why do some people prioritize achieving their dreams over seeking God's guidance, and how can they strike a balance between the two? (Follow God)
11. How can one discern the implementation strategy for their dreams and visions from God, and why is it important to ask for direction? (Follow God)
12. Can you share a personal experience where you learned the importance of seeking God's direction before executing a plan, and how did it impact your journey? (Follow God)
13. How can we discern between the dream God gave us and the desires that are corrupted by the devil? (Fight dream-killers)
14. What are some strategies we can use to overcome the dream killers in our lives, especially those close to us? (Fight dream-killers)
15. How can we balance contentment with our current achievements and the pursuit of greater dreams and goals? (Fight dream-killers)

Chapter 3

1. How do you define excellence and what are some examples of excellence in different areas of life? How can we pursue excellence in our own lives and maintain it as we progress in our personal and professional journeys? (The Spirit of Excellence)
2. What is the Spirit of excellence and how does it differ from regular excellence? How can we cultivate this spirit in our own lives and what role does our faith play in developing it? (The Spirit of Excellence)
3. How can we balance our pursuit of excellence with self-care and avoiding burnout? What are some strategies for maintaining a healthy balance and avoiding the pressure to constantly strive for perfection? (The Spirit of Excellence)
4. What role do spiritual and moral values play in achieving excellence, according to Daniel's story? Can one be excellent in a secular sense while still maintaining spiritual values? (Daniel)
5. How do knowledge, skill, understanding, and wisdom work together to produce excellence, as exemplified in Daniel's life? Are there other ingredients necessary for excellence that are not mentioned in the text? (Daniel)

6. How can one maintain excellence over a long period of time, as Daniel did in his career? What are some challenges that may arise when trying to sustain excellence, and how can they be overcome? (Daniel)
7. How can one cultivate a mindset that values excellence? Are there any practical steps one can take to change their perspective towards excellence? (Value excellence)
8. How can leaders foster a culture of excellence in their teams or organizations? What are some effective strategies for promoting and reinforcing excellence as a core value? (Value excellence)
9. How can one train their mind to think thoughts of excellence, and what are some practical steps to achieve this? (Think excellence)
10. How can one cultivate a culture of excellence in their workplace, community, or organization, and what role does individual thinking play in achieving this? (Think excellence)
11. What are some of the benefits and drawbacks of formal education versus self-study when it comes to acquiring knowledge and achieving excellence? Which approach do you think is more effective for most people, and why? (Learn excellence)
12. How does having a good understanding of a subject or field contribute to success and making meaningful

contributions, as seen in the examples of historical figures and contemporary individuals mentioned in the book? (Learn excellence)

13. How important is it to have a mentor in developing professional skills? What qualities should one look for in a mentor? (Learn excellence)

14. Why is seeking feedback and being open to criticism an important part of achieving excellence? How can we ensure that we are receiving constructive feedback that helps us to grow and improve, rather than just criticism that brings us down? (Do excellence)

15. Are the rewards of excellence worth the effort and sacrifices required to achieve it? How can we balance the pursuit of excellence with other important aspects of our lives, such as family, friends, and leisure activities? (Reap & enjoy excellence)

Chapter 4

1. How can understanding that God operates in different time zones for different people bring peace and comfort in our personal and professional journeys?

2. Why is it difficult for humans to reconcile the concept of time with God's plan for our lives? How can we learn to trust in God's timing, even when it doesn't

align with our own plans and expectations? (God's timing)

3. How does impatience affect decision-making, and what are some examples of historical figures or modern-day individuals who have made poor decisions due to impatience? How can we cultivate patience in our own lives, especially when it comes to waiting for God's plan to unfold? (God's timing)
4. How can individuals balance the benefits of healthy comparison, such as motivation and goal setting, with the negative emotions that can arise from unhealthy comparison, such as jealousy and low self-esteem? (Comparison)
5. In what ways can society promote individuality and discourage unhealthy comparison, particularly in an age where social media platforms encourage constant comparison and the creation of idealized versions of oneself? (Comparison)
6. How can social media impact our self-perception and what strategies can we use to avoid negative comparisons and maintain a healthy perspective? (Cure for Comparison)
7. Why is focusing on our own journey and progress important in achieving personal fulfillment and growth, and how can we practice self-compassion in the process? (Cure for Comparison)

8. How can believers ensure that they are seeking God's guidance and direction for their lives instead of following popular choices or the advice of others? (Follow God)
9. In what ways can we encourage others to seek God's plan for their lives, especially when it comes to making important decisions like choosing a career path or making a major life change? (Follow God)
10. How do you balance the idea of God never being late with the reality of difficult waiting seasons in life? How can we trust God's timing when it doesn't seem to align with our expectations? (Restoration of time)
11. The idea of God restoring what has been lost in waiting is a powerful one. How have you seen this play out in your own life or in the lives of others? How can we hold onto hope and trust that God will restore what has been lost? (Restoration of time)

Chapter 5

1. What are some practical ways that individuals can improve their ability to maintain focus in a world full of distractions and competing priorities?
2. How can leaders use the power of focus to drive success and inspire their team to stay committed and motivated towards achieving a common goal?

Can you provide examples of successful leaders who demonstrated this ability?

3. How can we differentiate between healthy fear and the kind of fear that distracts us from achieving our God-given goals? Are there any practical steps we can take to overcome the latter type of fear? (Distractions – Fear)

4. How do we guard our minds against the distractions of fear? What role does faith play in overcoming fear, and how can we grow our faith to a level that can stand against the distractions of fear? (Distractions – Fear)

5. How can we distinguish between harmless pleasures and destructive distractions? Are there any clear indicators that can help us recognize when we are crossing the line and allowing pleasure to take over our purpose? (Distractions – Flesh)

6. Are there any effective strategies or techniques that can help us overcome distractions caused by pleasure or addiction? How can we stay focused on our goals and resist the temptation to indulge in things that bring us temporary pleasure but hinder our long-term success? (Distractions – Flesh)

7. How can individuals overcome the feelings of hopelessness, helplessness, and depression that often come with failure in major aspects of life, such as a

career, financial stability, or personal relationships? (Distractions – Failure)

8. What can society do to help prevent suicide as a result of failure and depression, especially in young individuals who may feel overwhelmed by the pressures of success? (Distractions – Failure)

9. Can determination be taught or is it an innate quality? How can individuals cultivate and maintain determination in the face of challenges and setbacks? (Focus Enhancers – Determination)

10. How does determination contribute to success in academic and professional pursuits? Can determination be a greater predictor of success than intelligence or talent? How do individuals balance determination and self-care when facing obstacles along their journey? (Focus Enhancers – Determination)

11. How can discipline be developed and maintained in individuals, especially in the face of distractions and temptations that may arise along the way? (Focus Enhancers – Discipline)

12. How important is discipline in achieving success, and what are some practical steps individuals can take to cultivate discipline in their lives? (Focus Enhancers – Discipline)

13. Why do you think diligence is often overlooked or undervalued in society, despite being an important

trait for success in many areas of life? (Focus Enhancers – Diligence)
14. Can diligence be learned, or is it something that people are born with? What are some ways that someone can develop diligence as a habit? (Focus Enhancers – Diligence)
15. In what ways do you think modern technology affects our ability to focus and experience the rewards of focus mentioned above? Are there ways in which technology can be used to enhance focus and productivity, or is it mostly a hindrance?

Chapter 6

1. How do you determine the right season to make a crucial decision in life? Can making a decision after the right season still have a positive impact?
2. How do you develop the tenacity, confidence, and courage to make important decisions in life, especially when faced with great setbacks and challenges? What role does faith play in making difficult decisions?
3. How can having a clear vision for your life help you make better decisions, and how can you develop a vision if you currently don't have one? (Vision)

4. In what ways can a lack of vision hinder personal growth and success, and how can individuals overcome this obstacle to achieve their goals? (Vision)

5. What steps can someone take to renew their mind and align their thoughts with God's will, especially when struggling with negative influences and low self-esteem? (Mind)

6. How can individuals improve their self-efficacy, and what impact can this have on achieving their goals and fulfilling their purpose in life? (Mind)

7. How can we differentiate between purposeful pressure and negative pressure in our lives, and what strategies can we use to channel pressure towards purpose? (Pressure)

8. In what ways can societal expectations and pressure from others influence our decision-making processes, and how can we overcome these pressures to stay true to our purpose and vision? (Pressure)

9. How can we help teenagers and young adults navigate the negative effects of peer pressure, and what can parents and guardians do to support their children in making purposeful decisions in the face of external pressures? (Pressure)

Chapter 7

1. What does it mean to "faith it till you make it"? Can you give examples of situations where this approach could be helpful or harmful?
2. How do you cultivate and strengthen your faith? What practices or actions do you take to maintain your trust in God or a higher power, especially during difficult or uncertain times?
3. How does faith intersect with risk-taking? Can you think of a time when you took a big risk based on your faith, and what was the outcome? How did that experience impact your perspective on faith and risk-taking?
4. How does one activate their faith in Jesus Christ, and what role does this faith play in navigating one's journey in life? (Activate)
5. How can we strengthen our faith in God to conquer the challenges and obstacles we face in the world? (Activate)
6. What is the relationship between faith and salvation, and how does having faith contribute to our ability to reach heights beyond our human limitations? (Activate)
7. What are some practical ways to increase our faith and move from "little faith" to "great faith"? (Level)

8. How does fear affect our level of faith, and what can we do to overcome fear and increase our faith? (Level)
9. Can you share a personal experience when you had to exercise strong faith to overcome a difficult situation? How did that experience impact your faith? (Level)
10. In your experience, what has been the most effective way to develop and grow your faith? Is it through prayer, meditation, confession, obedience, thanksgiving, or patience, or is it a combination of these practices? Share examples of how these practices have helped you increase your faith. (Develop)
11. How can one maintain their faith during difficult times, such as when faced with illness, loss, or financial challenges? What role do prayer, scripture, community, and personal experiences play in keeping one's faith strong and resilient during such times? (Develop)
12. In what ways does faith impact our daily lives and decision-making? How can we ensure that our faith is not just a theoretical concept, but something that guides our actions, choices, and relationships? How do we strike a balance between faith and reason in our personal and professional lives? (Develop)

NOTES

Chapter 1: Find God

1. Philip, Craig, & Dean. (2006). Awake My Soul. On Top of My Lungs [Album]. Reunion Records
2. Conquer Series. (n.d.). 15 Mind-Blowing Statistics about Pornography and the Church. Retrieved from https://conquerseries.com/15-mind-blowing-statistics-about-pornography-and-the-church

Chapter 2: Fish Big

1. Longstaff, William D. "Take Time to Be Holy." 1882nd ed.
2. The Martins. "The Promise." New Day, 1999

Chapter 3: Fly with Excellence

1. Swindoll, Charles R. "Charles R. Swindoll Quotes." BrainyQuote, Xplore, www.brainyquote.com/quotes/charles_r_swindoll_130092.
2. National Center for Education Statistics, "Characteristics of Public and Private Elementary and Secondary Schools in the United States: Results From the 2017-2018 National Teacher and Principal Survey," March 2020

3   Marzano, R. J. "The Art and Science of Teaching," 2007

Chapter 4: Follow your Time zone.

1   Burchard, Brendon. "The Motivation Manifesto: 9 Declarations to Claim Your Personal Power." Carlsbad, CA: Hay House, 2014.

Chapter 5: Focus on your Focus

1   Kruse, K. (2012, July 16). The 7 Habits of Highly Effective People: Powerful Lessons in Personal Change. Forbes. Retrieved from https://www.forbes.com/sites/kevinkruse/2012/07/16/the-7-habits/?sh=89f4ba639c6d
2   Iacocca, L. (n.d.). BrainyQuote. Retrieved February 27, 2023, from https://www.brainyquote.com/quotes/lee_iacocca_381858
3   Jeff and Sher Easter. "New Day" My, Oh My, 2002

Chapter 6: Firmly Make Decisions

Chapter 7: Faith it.